Zen
and the Art
of Sailing
Willow

JASON BOYD

COPYRIGHT
PUBLISHING
9781796814941

This book is dedicated to my family,
John and Mary Boyd,
Selene Boyd, Jonathan and Stephanie Boyd,
Brittany Boyd, Jason (JC) Boyd, Albert (Al)
Forsyth, Mark McLean and Traci Helton for their
fear, love and support.
I am truly blessed to have each of you in my life.

Special thanks to David DuPont for his expert
guidance and to Kimberly Kratz for the editing of
my words.

Introduction

In Point Lookout, Maryland, on a windy summer day in 1979 just after I'd finished the eighth grade, I stepped onto a sail boat for the first time.

My sister's best friend Debbie accompanied me on the 10-foot sunfish. On the cusp of becoming a man, I hadn't learned much about girls to that point, but I was doing my best to impress her. As we boarded the small sailboat, I watched others and made mental notes as they launched their sunfishes. It looked so easy. I was sure I could handle it.

With our life jackets on, Debbie and I sat down in the sunfish ready to shove off into the 15-20 mile an hour winds. With a push, I raised the sail. A gust of wind filled the sail and we were off!

Excited, we both looked at each other and laughed, saying how great it felt. We looked ahead just as the sunfish sideswiped the only pole in sight. The sail snagged the sign on the pole and didn't want to let go. I did everything I could think of, but of course, nothing worked—mostly because I knew nothing at all about sailing.

Stuck and embarrassed, without a clue as to what to do, I sprang into action grabbing the pole at the bottom of the sail. I put my foot against the big pole that stuck out of the water and pulled and pulled. The stubborn sail released the sign, and I almost fell over but sat down hard instead. Relieved and a little proud that I had managed to unsnag it, I looked at Debbie. We both laughed it off as the little sunfish took off again. I'm not sure what I did but the little sailboat spun around with a mind of its own and lodged itself right against the pole again!

This time it stuck. Really stuck. No matter how hard I pulled, she would not let go. I heard voices yelling at me from the dock as the sail tore against the sign.

"Stop!"

"Wait!"

People were coming out to save me. I wanted to sink into the water so no one could see me. That was the last time I was on a sailboat.

Now it's July 2018, and I am at a crossroads. I can keep crawling around in attics to work on air conditioners or I can take a leap of faith. I choose to leap to save my life. I'm 53 years old, weigh a hefty 315 lbs., and I am diabetic with high blood pressure having survived two heart attacks and two heat strokes. My doctor says I have to change my work—find something else, a different way to make a living. He says I won't survive another heart attack or another heat stroke.

I have just purchased my first sailboat, a 31-foot, 1964 Prout Ranger Catamaran, one of three in the United States. She's beautiful; resembling an elegant tank (if there is such a thing.)

I bought her from Yan, an 80-year-old, true salt of a man who had to hang up his sailor's cap due to a condition in his eyes called macular degeneration of the retina. Basically he's legally blind. On the phone, Yan had a kind, reassuring voice and with concern asked questions to insure I was up to the task of sailing her. I told him I had had some experience, (I didn't elaborate) and that I was planning to take her to the Bahamas after I had gained more experience.

Yan told me about *Willow* in great, caring detail. He had been prepping her to sail to the Bahamas, but his rapidly deteriorating vision forced him to let her go. I immediately liked Yan and set a date to see *Willow*.

Yan gave me the name of a modestly priced, though surprisingly comfortable and elegant Airbnb called The Georgia Way where I could stay on the night before he and I met. The owner, Christie, was warm and welcoming. She had two cold beers waiting on me when I arrived. We sat out on her quaint front patio talking as people walked by along the moonlit street. It seemed as though everyone who walked by knew her.

Christie shared with me her history and that of the house. She had created the Airbnb out of grief and love after the loss of her husband and father of her children. Creed 'Skip" Frazier IV passed away suddenly from a heart attack. He was an avid fisherman and loved the Outer Banks. Christie brought their children to the New Bern home, a mere five-minute walk to the water and close enough for her boys, Creed V and Reece, to explore and enjoy the water as their father did. I enjoyed my stay and recommend it to anyone who needs a place to stay when visiting New Bern.

The next morning, I met up with Yan. I liked Yan even more in person. He had white flowing hair and a long, white beard; his darkened skin conveyed his 50 years on the water, sailing. He dressed with the casualness reserved for those in no hurry. His downward curved pipe never left his side.

This is the true story of the seven-day sail that followed. I hope you enjoy it as much as I did.

***

DAY ONE

I spent most the day running around purchasing supplies and making a conscious effort to avoid cigarettes, alcohol, candy, chips or soda. I wanted to change my life, although I did bring a cheap bottle of wine to celebrate completion of the passage. My list was short.

Straw cowboy hat
Sunscreen SPF 30
Chapstick SPF 30
Celery
Dozen bananas
8 avocados
18 eggs
8 fresh pork patties
8 cans of smoked herring
8 cans of kippered herring
Box of club crackers
Sriracha mayo
Louisiana hot sauce
Mustard
Fresh green beans
Brussel sprouts
Squash and zucchini
Gallon of baby water (I needed the jug to put the oil in)
20 lb. of ice

Half gallon of almond milk, and as always, the old standbys: a loaf of bread, and peanut butter and jelly. Oh! And liquid coffee creamer!

My brother had given me a stovetop espresso maker with fresh ground coffee, and I was looking forward to enjoying my first cup of coffee on *Willow*. My mom had given me a club-warehouse sized box of Velveeta cheese, but I took one of the small blocks and left her with the rest. There's no way I could have eaten eat all that.

I had also wasted four hours looking for a bracket that would lower the motor. Yan had strongly suggested that I lower it because the small waves in the bay would cause the motor blades to cavitate resulting in negligible forward motion.

When I realized that the $300 bracket that I had purchased from West Marine (an hour and a half drive away) would not work, I took it to the local marine store. But they sent me to their sister store to return the bracket. I was not happy that it used up my last bit of cash, so I was glad to get the money back.

I hurried to snatch up Yan. We headed back to an old boat shop where I had seen a bracket earlier that I thought I could make work. After gladly whipping out $50 for a used motor bracket, we were on our way to drop off the supplies at *Willow*.

Next, we had to drop off the rental truck at the airport. At midnight the week before, when I had picked it up, the truck was the only option. Eager to get going, I had charged it to my debit card and left the car rental with a lot less money than I had planned. I almost cried when I saw the rental bill. I tried to exchange the truck for a small car when I arrived at my parents' place in Maryland to no avail.

Excited, I couldn't wait to get back to the boat. Around 6 p.m., Christie, owner of The Georgia Way, an Airbnb, dropped us off beside the locked gate. Yan unlocked it and we marched towards the transport boat. He would motor us out to the waiting *Willow*. We talked the entire ride out.

"Remember to drop the motor a few inches. It will move a lot quicker. If not, the small waves in the bay will make the going slow. The bridges are on channel 16," Yan instructed.

"When approaching a manned bridge, simply say, 'this is the boat *Willow* requesting an opening.'"

"Some of the bridges have top-of-the-hour openings, some on the half hour. Don't forget, you need to change the oil in the outboard before you go very far. There's a hand oil pump on the port side. You'll find it near the oil."

"You should consider scraping the bottom of the boat. That will help her sail quicker. There is a two-foot scraper in the port side near the oil and a heavy, medium-size one as well. Just anchor up in two to three feet of water and get to scraping."

"I had planned to do it by now," he said, "but I'd have to do it by myself, and I can't do it alone."

I asked him whether his son could help. Peaking my curiosity, Yan explained that while his son often helps him out, in this case, he just couldn't. Yan just shrugged and said, "My son doesn't mind scraping the hull around the sharks, 'cause he can deal with what he can see. It's what he can't see that he can't deal with."

"What do you mean?" I asked.

"He don't like alligators much."

I glanced back at him.

"Alligators?" I asked.

"Yes," he replied.

"You can't see them coming. I just don't think about them," he added.

As I looked around the brackish water, I thought, "Yeah, I see his point."

"Oh, and there's a ferry. Don't expect them to change course even if you have the right of way."

Continuing he gave me a few more pointers. "Don't sail at night, period. When you drop anchor for the evening, there's a light that you need to hang. It's required when at anchor. We generally hang it on the boom above the cockpit for lighting as well. I'll show it to you when we get there."

"If you need to call the Coast Guard, never say "Mayday'. It's a bad thing to do if you're not dying. So, make sure you're dying if you are going to call a 'mayday.' If you just need information, just state what you need, and they will tell you what radio channel to go to for a response."

He talked. I listened. I needed to. I needed all of the experience I could absorb.

We boarded *Willow* and Yan started to collect his personal items. I found a Phillips head screwdriver and unscrewed the screw that held down the hand-carved ironwood monkey with the bright eyes and took it off the shelf. It weighed heavy in my hands. Unusually heavy. I handed the monkey to him and he looked at it fondly.

"It's ironwood," he said.

It came from the smallest atoll island in Micronesia named Namoluk where he'd spent three years. Home to 250-300 people at that time, Namoluk (which means "lagoon in the middle") has a land mass of a mere quarter mile wide by four and a half miles long. There Yan had learned a language that roughly only 2,000 people in the world know today.

Before Yan left the island, the chief had hand-carved the ironwood monkey and given it as a gift of protection for his adventures on the water. Yan explained that the Islanders worship deities, not God. The monkey was their deity of protection. It had served him well having looked after him and kept him sailing safely for the remainder of his sailing years.

Yan looked at me and smiled, his blue eyes sparkling as he gathered all of his things and placed them on the transport boat. There was so much more I wanted to ask him— answers that would give me something to look forward to.

He pulled out the light that adorns the boom at night and made sure it worked. Handing it to me, he instructed me to put it somewhere close.

"Make sure you hang it from the boom here in the cockpit at night when you anchor," he said.

"One last thing," he said.

"A toast. A shot of rum to say goodbye to *Willow*."

He scrambled back inside the cabin as if he was in his mid-twenties and returned with two plastic cups, each with a significant amount of rum. He handed me one, raised his, and toasted, "Goodbye, *Willow*."

Yan gulped the shot. I did the same. It was warm, strong and burned going down. It took all I had not to cough. He said he'd never found better in all his travels than this Haitian island rum and he drank two shots every evening. He'd leave the rest with me.

As he turned to go, I told him that I appreciated it. I wanted to ask him more questions about his 50 years of sailing, but I hesitated. Stopping for a moment, he turned to me and wished me fair winds and following seas. We shook hands and he climbed aboard the motor boat and cast off the ropes. He turned the boat away and slowly disappeared in the distance. He never looked back.

I wondered what it was like, what my life would soon be like. Would the two compare? Would it be the adventure or the freedom that I'd sought? Hopefully a melody of both. Time would tell. Suddenly, I felt alone, staring at the last place I had seen Yan before he disappeared.

In the weeks before, I had spoken to Yan many times on the phone, talking about *Willow*, but I found myself more interested in Yan and his stories than *Willow*. But that was only because I had known I was going to buy her the moment I had received his wife's email informing that the sailboat's name was *Willow*. I knew she was mine (for reasons I'll later explain.)

I had focused our conversations more about years of sailing. By the time we met, I was not only looking forward to meeting *Willow*, but meeting her owner as well. From the moment I met Yan in person, he was more than I had expected.

Though thin, Yan was muscular for his 80-year-old frame. Eyes blue and crystal clear, flowing white hair, the curved pipe. The sailor's, sailor. His tan, aging skin cloaked the young body that appeared to be stuck in its prime, the result of good genes, good sailing or even the two shots of rum before bed. (I opt for sailing. Truth be told, I opt for the rum as well.)

There I stood, not exactly a sailor's sailor. Not anything yet. But I was willing to become whatever the future needed me to be. I stood a bit taller on *Willow*, a bit more pride in my own sails.

And there we were, tied to a mooring ball, stranded, no dingy, totally alone. I couldn't have been happier! I figured it would take seven days to sail her from New Bern, North

Carolina to Tall Timbers, Maryland. Well, actually, Andover Estates/Valley Lee, but close enough for planning this trip. Seven days if all went well.

My heart soared. I was laughing and smiling. My arms outstretched, my face tilted up towards the sky.
"Yes! Yes! Yes! I have finally done it!" I thought.
This was the beginning of a life I had only dreamed of for as long as I could remember. Singing and humming, I happily unpacked my supplies, tucking everything in its place, even making the bed, putting pillow cases on—the whole nine yards. Just enjoying the feeling as if it were the first day of the rest of my life. I felt, young again, full of energy and excitement I had not felt in a very long time. It was if I had fallen in love. Alas, I may have.

I had about three hours before nightfall. Feeling no rush to put things away, time seemed to have slowed my life down just so I could savor this moment. I would put up a little bit, then stand up on deck, and cross my arms to lean on top of the cabin just to look.

Willow was beautiful to me. A 31-foot long by 15-foot wide catamaran of fifty-four years, she appeared still in her prime. Built in 1964, her extra thick hull pre-dated the understanding of the strength of fiberglass. Freshly painted white with light blue, rough areas where you'd place your feet, she was a tank—a safe, stable home at least for the next seven days.

Yan said that the wind would be blowing from the wrong direction for the next few days, that I should wait for it to change direction. I had agreed with him, but now, I wasn't so sure I could wait. Leaving now would be foolish. So, I put the things away and relaxed. I was in no hurry. Tomorrow could be a different story.

Everything in its place, I sat on the bench cushion at the sailboats wheel on the port side. Placing my hands on it, I turned it to the left, then the right as I watched how the rudders responded with only a small amount of resistance. Yan had developed the steering system with Kevlar rope, instead of cable. I could see the thought that he had put into the refit.

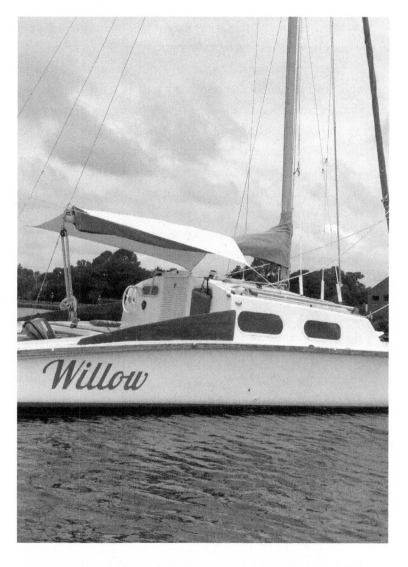

I noticed a rope that had one of those knots in it. You know, the one that goes around the tree, then down the rabbit hole. Something like that. I sat for a while trying to copy the knot with another rope. When I finally did it right, I untied the knot. I did this over and over again until I had memorized the steps.

I set it down and came back to it several times until I had it down pat. As silly as it sounds, a small sense of pride coursed through me. It was a simple pleasure. Hopefully it would be the first accomplishment of many to come.

As the day turned to night, I pulled out the small 12-volt light and adorned the boom with it. It felt ceremonial like a ritual. I immediately thought of the many people, unknown to me, who might have sat under this particular boom, sharing this type of moment. Surreal, in a pleasant way.

I wished that *Willow* could speak to me, share her own stories and adventures, the good and the bad. Instead she lay quietly on the water like a true lady, unwilling to give up any of her past or her secrets, comfortable in her silence. She let me decide our fate alone.

The bright full moon mimicked early morning and seemed to outshine the nearby brightly lit marina though a brisk wind blew through a well-lit park about 200 feet behind *Willow*. I could see people jogging and couples sitting on benches, watching me as I watched them. Perhaps they were wondering where I was headed or dreamed of embarking themselves maybe...picturing themselves sailing away, or not. I got lost in my thoughts.

I don't yearn to be them
As they may yearn to be me
I think not of how their evening will or will not be
For I know their daily woes
As well as it knows me
So, it is the tomorrow me that I yearn to be
Not them
Not there, not anywhere
But here on the water with *Willow*

Sailing away
To whatever fate we may await
We grow tired of the same scenery
The same footsteps
The same time this, the same time that
Always knowing where we'll be
Knowing what lies ahead
We are tired of feeling kinda dead
So, I've found it's my time
To cast off the lines
To lift the mainsail
I'm leaving it all behind
And watch
As I become neither the follower nor the leader
As I am now, both student and teacher
Lover and heart breaker
Slave and owner
Loving equinox while learning paradox
Seemingly no longer of my kind
A different breed
A different mind
The woman's woman
The man's man
Different than we were on land

It's a quiet evening long after sunset, the wind nearly imperceptible. In the distance I heard a "Ting, Ting. Ting." I could hear the unsecured halyards lines slapping against the aluminum masts, over and over again and I understood what Yan had said about the halyard and how he dislikes marinas. "It's just lazy and disrespectful to the others around you," he'd said.

Yan showed me the halyard and the bungee that kept it tight in the quiet hope that I would keep *Willow* respectful. I had made a mental note of it.

Smiling, I patted the top of the cabin, stepped in, slid the hatch shut and closed the two swinging saloon doors. Stepping to the starboard, ducking as I went the few steps down, I turned left, stood up and smacked my head on the four bolts that hold the handrail secured to the deck. Rubbing my fingers over my scalp, I checked for blood. It sure *felt* like there should have been.

Moving forward, I had to step over the entry bulkhead to the main cabin while I ducked to make it through the opening...quite an uncomfortable feat for me. I knew *Willow* was a bit small for me, but I had resigned myself that it would eventually become a bit more comfortable as I would eventually shrink with age.

Crawling up and into the bed, I flopped down on my back. The three hatches in the cabin top, one just below my feet, one at my mid-section and one just above my head were open and the wind found its way to me. About eighteen inches square, they were held open by springs. I just lay there looking up, taking it all in. I could see the clear, night sky, stars abundant. The full moon appeared to be staring back at me. The air flowing from the anchor locker soothed as well.

As I lay there blanketed in the peacefulness, my mind drifted, sailing the seven seas with *Willow,* changing my world, changing me. Thoughts of endless possibilities flooded my mind. I don't know when I feel asleep, but *Willow's* gentle rocking let me drift off.

***

DAY TWO

I woke early, around 5:00 a.m.

Sleep had found me easily and I felt refreshed and energized. The wind, still blowing from the wrong direction, had me feeling a little disheartened. I looked toward the railroad bridge, then the swing bridge and the large bridge in the distance.

"Wait until the wind changes," Yan had said.

"A day or two and it will shift. When it does, she will be able to sail. Otherwise you will have to motor into the wind, and it will be slow going unless you lower the motor like we talked about."

I made coffee on the small, two burner propane stove. The brewing coffee smelled unusually rich. Like the taste of food over a campfire, I soon discovered that anything cooked on board *Willow* seemed more flavorful—better for whatever reason.

I took my heart pills, shots for the diabetes, and poured myself a cup of coffee. I sat in the cockpit on the long bench and watched the sunrise. Like most working-class people, at this time of day I'd normally be getting ready for work, fueling up my truck, or driving from here to there without time to stop to enjoy "the little things." I'd rarely see the sun come up like this.

It's taken me years to get to the point where I've begun to learn that "little things" like precious moments, heartfelt feelings, truer things—those experiences that don't involve money are actually big and important.

I watched the high bridge as the beams of light from vehicles, obscured by its structure, shot into the dark sky until they reached the peak of its climb to start their descent, fading into an endless stream. I thought of the people driving those cars who are just like me; those lucky enough to enjoy the jobs to which they were headed.

"They are the winners for now," I told myself.

I have suffered that same fate, comfortable in my own uncomfortableness, as years of a job extracted their toll, turning my body and mind into something foreign, broken and numb. In my view, those who hate what they do for a living will excel in the future. Over time, their fear of change will lessen as the sheer hatred of staying on the job will eventually overpower that fear. The need for something better will coincide with the will to make it obtainable.

Sipping coffee, I looked below the bridge at the boats docked and those held by mooring balls.

"It's peaceful," I thought.

I looked around for alligators, but I didn't see any. They are there. I was sure. Thoughts of pulling into a shallow spot in the dark water and scraping the bottom gave me the chills. I knew that I would avoid doing that.

"Just don't think about them," Yan had said.

With the sun out, the night's coolness quickly faded. The slight breeze didn't ease the heat and soon the cabin became stifling, which eliminated the option of going inside.

"Okay," I thought to myself, "you'll just have to get used to it."

I decided to motor around a bit to get a feel for her. I pushed the button to tilt the motor down into the water, pumped the bulb to prime the fuel, pulled the choke, and then pushed the start button. The motor sprang to life. I untied the bow from the mooring, returned to the cockpit, put the motor in gear and gave it a little twist as we began to move.

For my first time driving her, I set the motor for a straight run and used the boat's wheel and rudders to steer. (I'd never taken her for a test run or even raised the sail. I just bought her.) She was exactly what I needed: bare boned, no air conditioning, no water maker, nothing fancy, and not much to break down—a simple sailboat for a simple person.

I motored around, twisted the throttle and increased her speed. I noticed the open train trestle bridge. I didn't give it a second thought and set a course right to it. Yan's words came to me.

"Always go on the side of the building where they can see you."

I shifted position and slowed to a third throttle, motoring through and into a big marina. Slowing to an idle, I admired the larger boats. A scant few were *Willow's* size. I thought about the size and comfort of the larger boats: the air conditioning, ice makers, refrigerators, and water makers which all led to the need for a generator. All of that would require maintenance and problems which in turn would lead to a higher cost.

I patted her cabin top, thankful that I had waited to make the right choice. So many other boats after which I had lusted had beautiful, long elegant lines, and stunning woodwork. They would have made me look good, accomplished even.

My ego had me hooked, making it difficult to be realistic. I finally determined that those were worth neither the constant maintenance nor the cost. I wanted to sail, not do upkeep all the time. I slowly motored up near the swing bridge.

"Oh, crap, gotta turn on the radio," I realized.

"Which channel? 16? I think so. What was I supposed to say?"

My mind went blank as I keyed the mike. It was 6:35 a.m.

"Hey y'all! Good morning! What time y'all open?"

Naw, that wasn't it.

"Top of the hour," came a reply.

"But it worked!" I thought to myself.

"Okay, thank you!" I replied, sure that I had said the wrong thing.

Turning around, I puttered back through the marina making a large, sweeping circle again and again.

People came out of their multi-level, million-dollar yachts in their pajamas and bathrobes and stood on the dock talking to each other, sipping coffee, and staring at me. Laughing, I did my best Forrest Gump wave. It took everything I had not to jump over the side and swim towards them just to catch their reactions.

I slowly made a large loop, this way then that way, getting a better feel for handling her. I couldn't let go of the wheel, for as soon as I did, she would immediately start to take a right turn. Thankfully, there was an autopilot somewhere in the boat. I could see why Yan had said it was impossible to sail her without it.

The humidity rose. I noticed cars stopped on the bridge and the bridge starting to raise.

"Why wait another day?" I thought.

As soon as the bridge became fully open, I motored through and aimed towards the center of the tall bridge. Seeing dark clouds in the distance, I understood why the yacht owners had looked at me the way they did. I was the only boat out on the water.

"Well, I thought, "gotta see what she can take, better now than later."

"To the swing bridge," I said.

"Thank you! Y'all have a great day!" I radioed.

"You too. Be careful out there," came the reply.

Rule one: Always be polite.

Rule two: Always say thank you.

Rule three: Be thankful.

I heard Yan's voice as clear as a buoy bell.

"Whenever you go under a bridge, go where the light is. That's the highest point. And, you'll notice horizontal wooden boards around the base of the bridge where you are to go. That will always be your path."

As I approached the bridge, I figured it was twice as high as my mast, so I would have no clearance problem. I motored through it like a pro. Even so, I have to admit I was still nervous.

Yan had been right. The small waves made the prop on the motor cavitate, slowing the forward movement, (not to mention the irritating sound the motor made each time the prop cut through the water's surface). It annoyed me because I could tell it wasn't supposed to make that cringe-worthy noise, and I worried that too much would cause motor damage at some point. At what point is too much? When it breaks, of course.

"Let's not wait that long," I thought.

"Don't forget to change the oil before you go too far," Yan's voice reminded me again.

I traveled three miles further past the bridge to a spot on the side where the depth finder measured about 18 feet of water. I tossed and set the anchor, returned to the port side and started looking for the oil and the pump. I found them both right where Yan said they would be.

"You put the small tube that protrudes from the hand pump down into the dipstick tube. Holding the tube-like pump, grab the knob and push it in and out. Kinda like a bicycle pump." I removed the cover from the outboard motor and did as Yan had said.

It drew the oil out and spit it into the gallon container I had brought. It was difficult to hold the pump, the jug, and to pump it at the same time, but I managed. With all of the oil out, it made a slurping sound.

"Great," I thought.

"Let's put the oil in."

I looked for a funnel but could not find one. I assumed that I could swap the hose-clamped ends of the handy oil pump and pump the oil back through the dipstick hole. I grabbed a screwdriver to swap out the ends.

"Perfection," I thought.

I tried to hold the gallon of oil, carefully tilting it so the large pick up tube would draw the oil up and push it into the small tube and into the motor. I pulled on the handle, felt it draw up the oil, and pushed down on the handle to force the oil down the smaller tube while balancing the half full gallon of oil. Like pushing molasses through a bar straw, the handle barely moved.

"Needs more pressure," I thought, but pushing harder was not the solution I had hoped for. There was no popping sound as I had expected.

Instead, I almost fell overboard because the handy little oil pump rapidly bottomed out, and since the plunger inside felt no resistance, the smaller end blew off spraying oil all over me, the engine, and *Willow*.

I watched in amazement as in slow-motion the smaller tube spring-boarded out of the engine, back flipped twice and slipped into the water making hardly a splash. I would have clapped for its perfect execution were it not for my current predicament.

I almost dove in after it, but my smart hand grabbed the motor and wouldn't let me. Yep, I know what you are thinking and you're right. How would I have gotten back in the boat had I dove in after it?

I set about digging out the ladder and placed it where Yan said it should go. I lowered myself over the edge and nervously I found myself at the bottom rung of the ladder in the warm, brackish water.

"Don't think about them," I half-scolded myself.

I started off the ladder to swim down, but my hand wouldn't let go. There was comfort in not letting go. So, I compromised like a child who finds himself clinging to the ladder at the deep end of the pool for the first time. I took a deep breath and forced myself feet first down towards the bottom, pushing at the bottom of the boat and letting go, going down as far as I could.

"Don't think about them," I thought again.

My ears started to feel the pressure. To my shock, the warm water turned to cold! I had still not reached the bottom. Suddenly, I decided I didn't care in the least to touch the bottom, much less find the tube that I desperately needed.

Until this occasion, I'd never panicked, but just then without even thinking, my hand (you know, the smart one) immediately started sweeping, swimming towards the surface as though it had a mind of its own.

"Don't think about them," I thought once again, but I couldn't help myself and I wanted out!

Breaking the water's surface, I felt sure that at any moment I would be chomped on, taken back under the water, reduced to a single bubble, gobbled up by some Lake Placid sized alligator.

"Blop."

In my head, I scampered up the ladder but in reality, I made my way up wishing that I was scampering. Wedged between the motor and the hull, I tried to get as much of me out of the water as I could, the imagined gator hot on my heels.

I made my way from the water by way of over-the-motor. It had been so much easier going down the ladder. I sat on the side of the cockpit, trying to catch my breath and looked around at the mess I had made. I scanned the dark water for signs of the gator that I shouldn't have been thinking about.

Oil covered everything, even the fuel tanks that I had moved out of the way. Oil everywhere except where it belonged; in the motor. I decided not to worry about it.

I needed to clean *Willow*. She was a hot mess and I had made her that way. I couldn't just wash her off. I knew that some oil had found its way into the water, but that was accidental. This mess, I'd have to sop up. I looked at the dark clouds that moved closer.

The hero of the day: toilet paper. It truly amazed me at how well it cleaned up the oil. The oil in the cracks? Just push down on the T.P. a bit and voilà! It's gone. No scrubbing required. And I enjoyed taking care of *Willow*, glad to clean her up.

In the process of restoring her beauty, I thought about the oil problem. Despite the lack of a funnel on board, I thought I knew what to do. During the final clean up, I opened the cooler and found my solution in a Sriracha mayo squeeze bottle.

I searched the cupboard to find a Ziploc bag. I opened the Sriracha, poured it all in, zipped it shut and tossed it into the cooler. I then cut out the bottom of the plastic bottle with a knife, took it to the sink and washed and dried it with a paper towel. I didn't want a single drop of water in the oil. I was sure it would fit in the oil dipstick hole, but I checked to be sure. Naturally, because I needed it to, it did not fit. Too big. I needed something smaller or something to make it smaller. I scrounged around through all the cabinets and little cubby holes until I had exhausted every option. After what felt like hours of searching, I saw the kitchen trash can that I had moved out of the way several times.

"Heck, why not?" I thought.

Digging through the trash I found what I needed on the very bottom: An old tube of painters caulk that Yan had tossed away. I held it up and smiled.

"Yeah, this will do."

I cut off the tip, cleaned and washed it. Then, over the propane stove in the galley, I heated both the end of the Sriracha bottle and the cut spout from the discarded tube of caulk and pushed them together. It held fast. Perfection. I set about putting the oil in the engine through the dipstick.

After that I pulled the two 6-gallon gas tanks and the propane tank from the transom to make way to scoot the outboard motor over. That way I could install the bracket that would lower the motor. In doing so, I came across a stowaway, a small, green tree frog. I didn't want to accidentally crush her or step on her and throwing her in the water was out of the question. I captured her, put her into the bag of celery and placed it on the cabin roof opened so she could catch a breeze and relax.

With the stowaway in her new quarters, out of harm's way, I went back to the motor. Unscrewing the motor mounts, I began the tough job of scooting the motor over about a foot. I was surprised. She was heavy despite her relatively small size. With a lot of effort, I finally had moved her out of the way.

Yan had given me two 2x12's; one about 14 inches long and the other about 16. I opted to go with the larger board, using it sideways to spread the load on the transom. (It made sense at the time.)

I set the bracket on the 2x12 and marked where I needed to drill the holes. I had bought a drill bit just for this occasion, along with stainless bolts, and nuts and washers. A cordless drill came with the boat.

I attached the drill bit and drilled the marked spots. With the holes drilled in the board, I moved to the transom. Leaning over, I held the board in place with one hand whilst trying to hold the drill steady to drill with the other. It's not as easy as it sounds.

After several attempts I finally had the first one drilled. I slid a bolt through and tightened it up. The next holes would be easier. Using both hands, I lay the drill bit into the hole in the board and drilled into the transom. Upon pulling the drill away, I heard a quiet "plop." One look at the end of the drill confirmed that the drill bit had fallen out.

"My drill bit. Lost at sea. It's probably right next to the tube that jumped ship," I thought.

Luckily for me, Yan had left a few drill bits with the sailboat and I quickly replaced the drowned one with another of similar size so I could drill and attach bracket to board and the board to the transom. I only lost one half-inch socket overboard, but I finished it all up with an adjustable without further incident. With the bracket in place, I attempted the difficult task of sliding the motor to its new home at the end of the bracket. With grunts and groans mingled with a few choice words, I finally managed despite its weight and the extra foot it stood away from the transom.

With the motor in its new home, I tightened down the motor clamps that secured the motor to the bracket and stood up to admire my handiwork. It actually looked like I knew what I was doing!

Pleased with myself and the time that it had taken, I started putting the propane and gas tanks back in place inside the open transom. By then it had begun to sprinkle rain. I was sweaty and hot, and the rain drops had a magnificent cooling effect. I pulled out some paper towels and started cleaning her up again. I eliminated all traces of the wood shavings and wiped down the tools I'd used to tighten up the bolts, for they were hers and needed to be treated as such.

Soon, *Willow* sparkled again. I stood in the middle of the deck, under the boom in the rain admiring her. I smiled and felt as though she smiled with me.

The rain thickened, not a heavy rain that makes it hard to see, but more than the sprinkle it had been. The wind picked up and the waves grew to 2 or 3 feet.

"Time to get going," I thought.

I started the motor and put it to a forward idle in the direction of the anchor. I worked myself over the edge to the side deck walking as quickly as I dared, holding onto the handrail as I went. I let the smart hand lead the way. When I made it to the bow, I dropped to my knees, crawled the six feet to the anchor locker and grabbed the anchor line that was tied to the huge cleat in the front dead center. She was starting to buck like a bronco just out of the gate.

With one hand holding the anchor line, I grabbed the steel cable running up to the mast and slowly stood up, legs spread wide to hold my balance as I pulled up the anchor as the boat idled into the small waves. This caused the boat to rock forward and aft while the waves knocked her side to side. As I pulled up the building slack, I came to the part where the anchor line had become tight. Using both of my hands in an effort to steady myself, I found that I could only pull the line upward when the boat moved in the downward direction. Then holding it fast I leaned back and locked my knees as the bow started to raise and the anchor started to let go of the bottom as the boat overtook the anchor line. I hurriedly pulled up the oddly heavy anchor as fast as I could.

When the anchor finally broke the water's surface, I could see a thick covering of grey mud on one side that felt like an extra 40 pounds. I looked around as I continued to drop the anchor in and out of the water to clear the mud off of it. We were fine, making a wide arch in the water away from land. So, I finished cleaning off the mud to avoid getting my girl *Willow* muddy.

With the anchor and chain cleaned, I stowed the anchor, line, and chain in the anchor locker and make my way back to the cockpit. I set *Willow* on a course towards the middle of the river. I enjoyed the feel of the cool rain on my hot skin. I steered slightly left as I made our way out. Reaching back, I twisted the arm of the motor and brought it to 3/4 speed. The motor responded instantly, and we moved at a small clip. I noticed that the motor did not cavitate at all when she was plowing through the waves.

Yan was right. It did make a difference.

"Perfect," I thought.

"We are underway."

The rain and wind had increased. I could see the shoreline with the piers but not much else. Visibility continued to decrease. I had motored about a mile when the motor made a strange, high-pitched sound along with a cavitating noise, then a strange gurgling. Startled by the sounds, I turned to look back quickly. In the precise place where the motor attaches to the bracket and the bracket attaches to the transom was a blank space.

The entire motor and bracket, MIA. POW. Prisoner of water.

Gone.

Disappeared.

Vanished!

My heart sank.

I almost threw up.

"What am I going to do now?" I wondered.

Then, I moved aft and looked down into the water. There was my little, overweight 9.9 Yamaha looking up at me, the gas line doing all it could to hold onto her.

I took all this in within a split second. My brain still tried to comprehend, but my smart hand was already on the move, lunging forward, and taking my entire body with it. It almost dove me over the edge but timed it just right.

In an instant I found myself sprawled out over the port hull dangling on the inside between the two hulls, holding onto this 9.9 and playing a game of "Bobbing for Alligators." Up and down the boat rose and fell in the steady rain. I had no idea where she was being steered. Luckily the motor had shut down.

"Thank God, I'm fat," I thought.

'Cause seriously, that's all that kept me from going over with the motor. Smart hand was not letting go.

Bobbing in, hold breath. Bobbing out, breathe a bunch. My heart pounded away as I sweat profusely even in the cool rain. My feet were spread, up in the air trying to maintain precious balance, an appearance reminiscent of a sea lion on one of those nature shows. The way those animals kinda roll their fat forward to move—well, that was me, only backwards. I'd kicked my feet up, awkwardly trying to lift my stomach up so I could push backwards to get my face out of the water. I needed to reposition myself to where my arm was the only thing hanging over the side. The other hand floundered around in a panic like a fish out of water, searching for support from the transom until it finally gripped and hung on, helping me to balance. I pushed myself up, level with the deck, flopping myself backwards.

"Just don't think about them," I commanded myself.

I still had no idea where *Willow* was headed. I didn't care, it wouldn't matter if I lost the engine. Through the prolonged efforts of kicking my legs, cursing, pulling and pushing, timing them with the rise and fall of the boat, I finally managed to lock my arm over the side. The arm that has the smart hand at the end of it shook uncontrollably.

With excruciating clarity, these shenanigans tested my shoulder's pain tolerance. My torn rotator cuff and past dislocations were not faring well. Like a blind lab mouse in a maze with a cheese prize, the other hand started flopping around in search of a rope.

I closed my eyes and tried to remember where everything was as the boat bobbed up and down, rain hammering staccato on me. Droplets landed in my ear, sweat stung my eyes, and the water tried to suck the engine out of my hand as each rise and fall of the boat tried to tear my shoulder from my body.

In a combination of agony and panic, I start laughing. I couldn't pick a better place for this to happen?
I felt around with my feet. There, on the edge of reach, a rope! I tried to pick it up with my toes, but just couldn't seem to get it. I still wondered where *Willow* headed. I finally managed to get the rope between my feet and tried to toss it up towards me. It just managed to wrap around my foot when I got a sharp Charlie horse.

I start to laugh and curse at the same time—a full-on oxymoron of comedic proportion. It really hurt. My body was in so much pain it don't know what to do. I tried to straighten out the leg, but it really was not cooperating, so I used the other leg to push it down, and I was not really surprised when the other leg started to cramp as well.

I managed to worm my way to my side, backed my heels against the side bulkhead and kept as much pressure on them as I could. I was able to see how the rope had wrapped around my foot. Through the cramps I managed to untangle it. Wedging the rope between my foot and the deck, every time the cramps let up, I attempted to scoot the rope towards me, inviting the cramps to return, and their performance did not disappoint.

Finally, I was able to reach the rope with a hand. Dragging it towards the transom, I dropped one end into the water. I had to scoot myself back towards the water so I could reach the motor with rope in hand. Again, I bobbed away and tried to fit the rope through the half-inch spot between the smart hand and the bracket. I waited until the boat dipped down to pull the engine up towards the waiting hand with the rope. Panting and shaking, the hand missed the first time. My smart hand lowered the motor waiting for the next wave to pick us up, only to lower us again. As we bobbed upward, I readied both hands making sure that I had about an inch of rope to push through, and prepared to bring up the motor with the other.

"Here we go."

The boat bobbed downward, and I heaved up on the motor. Shaking, I brought it up to the hand with the rope.

"Come on! Come on! Get in there!"

It went through.

"Oh, thank you, thank you. Thank you!" I said aloud.

I reached around to pull the rope through only for it to slip back out. I spewed obscenities. This happened several times, as did the stream of curses as my arm which held the motor shook uncontrollably. I wanted to let go as I felt my arm pulling away from my shoulder.

"One more time," (talking to myself, the motor, the rope, the hand, anything and everything) I said.

"Come on, come up, up, up, get in there!"
Missed! Screaming as I let the motor back down, my body began to give out. I could feel it.

"I have nothing left,"

"This has got to be it."

Again, "Come on baby! Come here!"

Missed. I scooted back to catch my breath while I still grasped the motor in my shaking hand.

"I can't do this."
I could feel tendons and muscles testing in my shoulder. For a brief moment I hung there.

Willow still bucked.

The rain still poured.

I barely hung on.

My mind raced.

"How bad do you want it? What's a little pain compared to a lifetime of change? You've been through worse pain, physically and mentally and you're going to let this way of life escape you?"

"This brass ring? It's so close and you've missed so many. Reach out and grab it."

"It's yours. Do this and you will never be here again."

I steadied my hand with the rope as best as I could, brought the rope to my mouth and grabbed the end with my teeth to pull a little more of a tail out. I imagined the motor bracket in my hand. I pictured the small gaps. Like a weight lifter trying to adjust his hands after a deadlift, I couldn't wiggle my fingers that held the motor to make more room for the rope. I tried to steady myself, breathe through the pain, to slow everything down. Timing was critical, measuring the up and down of the hull.

"Please, let this be it."

As the hull dropped in the waves, I pulled with all my might on the motor, screaming through the wind and rain.

"Come on! Come on baby! Get up here."

As I threaded the rope through the motor bracket, I held it there as the hull bounced up tearing at my shoulder. It felt like it was popping loose. I screamed. My hand held and I was able to grab the small rope and pull it through.

"Okay thank you, thank you. Now, one more time!"

I threaded the rope up and around the open transom to feed it back down to the smart hand to repeat. Every part of my body shook. I fed the rope through, bringing it up past my ear and dropped it down though the open transom again. Twice more I did this, each more difficult than the last. Finally, when there were three complete turns, I slapped my hand on the turns of rope at the top of the transom and let go of the motor. I grabbed the rest of the rope, wrapped it around and tied it off leaving the motor suspended in the water by the rope.

I pushed myself upright to take a look. She laid there about a foot under the water. I collapsed back onto the deck, shaking and holding my shoulder. I let the rain pelt me. It was a gully washer, a downpour, and *Willow* was like a horse bucking in its stall.

Lying on my back, looking up through the rain just trying to breathe I saw the clouds moving.

"We are still moving!"

I sprang to my feet. My heart still raced. I saw a pier not 20 yards away. *Willow* had made a huge right handed arch and we'd completely moved to the other side of the river on a collision course with a pier. I jumped up on the bench seat by the steering wheel and hopped over to run up the side of the boat. Doing so caused me to smack my toes on the rail and fall forward. Seeming of its own accord, my hand lunged for the handrail that runs down the top side of the cabin and grabbed onto it just as my feet flung over the side, scraping my shins along the way. I struggled against the pitching hull, as my body splayed, my feet dangling over the side.

My feet dropped in and out of the water with the bobbing of the boat. Gripping the handrail, I pulled myself up and crawled along the entire length on my knees, working with only one hand I made my way forward. A hand clutched to my chest, my shoulder screamed in protest as I fell onto the front deck and scrambled to pull the anchor out of the locker. The anchor stuck.

I glanced up.

"Too close," I knew.

I shook the anchor until it finally let go. Pulling it up, I stood as I turned towards the back of the boat. Taking two steps forward, I grabbed the steel cable that parallels up to the mast and hung tightly as I slung the anchor and chain back towards the stern away from the pier.

It felt my shoulder separate then pop back into place with terrible pain. I immediately stepped onto the line and looked forward.

"No, no, no, no, no," I shouted rapid fire as the front starboard hull began its eclipse under the pier.

The anchor line tightened. I pulled it with all of my energy, my streaming tears mixing with the rain. Awaiting fate, I watched as the starboard hull slid under the pier and I held my breath as I heaved on the anchor line watching the port cable that goes up to the mast tighten as it gave way to the pier.

The cable tightened, then I relaxed as *Willow* slowly receded in the opposite direction. I pulled one handed while twisting myself so the anchor line wrapped around my body, causing us to swing away from the pier. Then *Willow* crossed over the anchor. Tearfully I pulled it up and tossed it again ignoring my shoulder's protest to put increasing distance between us and the pier each time.

On the bow I continued this process as she bobbed up and down, until I no longer felt the danger of *Willow* drifting into anything. I finally set the anchor and collapsed on the deck trying to catch my breath as my heart pounded heavily in my ears. I couldn't move for a moment. I let the rain hit my face as I turned it side to side in a fruitless attempt to drain the rainwater from my ears.

I crawled back to the cockpit holding onto the rail the entire way to avoid a painful replay. When I finally made it, still trying to regain my bearings, I sat on the edge looking down at the outboard motor with the bracket still attached to it, knowing there was no way I could pull her into the boat by myself.

The gas line had let go at some point, so I started pulling the gas cans and propane tank back out again. I'd moved everything out of the way, and I wondered how to proceed. In frustration my hand tightened up on the ropes that were all wrapped up in pulleys at the end of the boom. I suddenly became excited.

"Pulleys...Boom! There we go!" I thought.

When Yan had shown me the items in the boat, I had seen what I thought was an equipment-repelling double loop. He had said that the special, lightweight alloy could probably pick up the whole boat if need be. I found it quickly and began to unhook the bottom pulley.

By then an emotional wreck I still shook and willed myself to stop. I couldn't afford to drop anything else overboard.

"It's time to get some water and relax a minute, nothing will change in the meantime," I thought.

The igloo cooler sat on the bench seat on the starboard side. I had to push my cup up against the cooler to steady my hand, but I couldn't push the knob hard enough to allow water to fill my cup. I was too shaky and had not the strength. I sunk down to my knees and rested my forehead against the cooler. Pushing my elbow to my side I leaned into it using my weight to push in the knob, and the water soon filled the cup. I tilted my head back as the rain cooled my face. I took a swig between breaths and poured the rest over my head. It was so cold it hurt, but it helped.

I felt my heart slow as my breathing eased. After some time, I no longer heard my heart beating in my ears. It took time and several cups of water until my shaking subsided. I started on the bottom pulley with painstaking care to avoid dropping anything overboard. I disconnected it from the rail and attached the alloy ring.

With that complete, I grabbed another rope and stretched out the pulley at the end of the boom to get as close to the motor as possible. I wrapped the rope back and forth between the alloy ring and the motor while shaking my head in effort to clear the rain from my ears. Tying off the rope, I tightened the pulley lines until the engine was raised enough to untie the rope that held the motor to the transom.

As the rain continued to punish, I began raising the motor out of the water as *Willow* bobbed up and down. Both the motor and bracket seemed to catch on everything which made it extremely difficult to maneuver. I wrapped another rope around the engine, tightened up the pulley lines, moved to the stern of the boat and pulled until the motor and bracket were free of the transom.

Once I returned to the cockpit, I pulled the pulley lines as far as they would go. They were not high enough to clear the bulkhead. I had to physically pick up the outboard motor so as to clear the bulkhead and move it where I'd have a secure space where I could work on it. With more effort than I thought I could muster, I managed to get the motor safely into the cockpit.

I sat down on the bench behind the steering wheel, shaking my head and laughed.

"Story of my life," I thought.

Sometimes I'm not sure how I would act if everything went smoothly. I would probably become paranoid, always anticipating what next thing might go wrong.

I drank the frigid water from the igloo cooler. Still, I drank some more until the brain freeze started. I put my tongue to the roof of my mouth to help it go away. Watching the rain fall into my cup between drinks, I briefly wondered what it would taste like to drink a glass full of rainwater.

"No time for that right now, gotta get on this engine," I thought.

I peeked in on my little stowaway frog. She appeared to be sleeping. I set the cup down and removed the engine cover. The front of the engine faced away from me. When I pulled the cover off, I saw a big, round, bright yellow cap clearly marked with one word: "OIL."

"Oh my God," I nearly died laughing.

"Well, now I know," I thought, knowing that I'd never forget that if I lived to be one hundred years old.
I pushed the start button on the engine. It turned about a tenth of a turn and locked up. (I know, but I had to try.)

"Okay, it has to have some water in it. Gotta get the water out," I said aloud to *Willow*.

I grabbed the bucket with the oil-soaked toilet paper and set it where I could drain the oil. I loosened the oil cap and picked up the motor until the mixture of oil and water started to pour out.

"Good shot, right into the bucket."

When all of the oil and water drained, I turned the motor around and set it back on the bulkhead, filled it and pushed the start button.

"No go. She's locked tight."

"Okay now, next?"

"Spark plugs."

I found the small socket set that I used to install the motor bracket. It had a spark plug socket. Wrong size.

"Okay, okay now. There has got to be one here somewhere," I said to myself.

I rummaged through all of the tool boxes and cabinets for nearly two hours. I went into the cabin to get out of the rain and by 4:00 in the afternoon, against my instincts and probably my pride, I considered breaking down to call Yan. Although I could still see where I started only the day before, I didn't see how Yan could help me considering his impaired vision, but I placed the call.

Yan answered the phone.

"Hello Yan!" I said, laughing.

"Well hello there Jason! I see you went ahead and headed out. How's that going?"

I laughed a bit and said, "Welllllllll, the engine fell off." Silence.

"What?"

"The engine fell off."

"Oh, my goodness, no way! I just can't believe that! What are you going to do?" he asked.

"Well, I'm going to fix it."

"You saved the motor? You mean you still have it?"

"Yes sir," I laughed, "It wasn't easy."

"I bet not. So, what's your plan?"

"Well, here's the problem. The spark plug socket I have doesn't fit and the adjustable is too big for such a tight space."

"Oh my. Did you check in the Honda box?"

"Remember? I dropped that off at my parents' house in Maryland with the Honda motor last week," I responded.

"Oh, my goodness. Let me think. Just give me a minute. Where abouts are you?"

"Well," I chuckled, "I can still see where I started; maybe three miles away."

"You didn't get too far, did you?"

"No," I laughed.

"I can't use the transport boat that we have been using. They pulled it out to work on it, but I may be able to get someone to come out there to help you," Yan said.

"I just need a spark plug socket or wrench. I think I can get her going again," I said.

"Wait a minute," he said.

"Step inside the cabin doors and turn around. At your feet are my 'quick needs supplies' in a Tupperware. There's a Ziploc bag that may have the wrench you need."

I had already pulled out all the Tupperware. I went through them again. Not there. Then I put my face on the floor and looked back into the hold where the Tupperware were kept. A Ziploc bag sat all the way in the back. I snatched it up and looked inside.

"Wahoo, it's here! And a set of new spark plugs. Gas filter as well. Thank you, thank you, thank you. I'll let you know how it goes," I told him.

"Good luck!" Yan replied.

"I hurried to the engine and removed the spark plug wires and then the spark plugs. I held my breath as I pushed the start button. The motor turned quickly. I hoped it would blow any leftover water through the spark plug holes. I put the new spark plugs in and pushed the start button. The motor locked up.

"Damn. Here we go again—pull the spark plugs, turn over the engine, put the plugs back in."

I checked the spark plug by placing it against the block, but it was barely visible, and I couldn't tell whether there was spark. Without thinking, I grabbed the spark plug and pushed the start button with the other. Yikes! That hurt. It nearly knocked me on my ass. Plenty of spark. I repeated the process until dark in an effort to get the remaining water out.

My phone rang. Caller ID said, "Yan."

I answered.

"How's it going?"

"I have spark," I said, "but nothing is happening."

"Did you drain the carb?"

"It has a carb?" I said (more as a question than a statement.)

With all the wires, I hadn't even seen the carburetor. I had assumed it had an electronic ignition.

"There's a small brass screw on the side. Only open it one turn. If you drop it, you'll never get it started," he told me.

"Okay, Yan. Thank you so much. It's getting dark and I'm spent. I'll mess with it in the morning," I said.

Filling my cup with ice cold water, I checked on my little celery-obscured stowaway. I was sure that the day's events may have caused her a bit of stress.

"She sure does sleep a lot," I thought.

I took the small anchor light from the cabin and adorned the boom with it. Closing the saloon doors behind me and sliding the hatch home, I made my way to the bed. As I climbed up, both my legs cramped. I flopped onto my back and pushed my feet against the inside of the hull, trying to ease the cramping. Straightening my legs, I locked my knees. Suddenly, my hamstrings cramped. My God, what a predicament.

I scrambled to get out of the bed so I could stand up to fight them. Exhaustion made for a rough night. The cramps dissipated at least until the middle of the night. Between the cramps and my concern about dragging the anchor, sleep eluded me. Several times I woke up to push my feet up to the low ceiling of the cabin, or to go out on the cockpit to check on whether *Willow* was dragging her anchor. Most of all, my shoulder ached miserably. No sooner would I fall asleep, then I would wake up concerned.

I don't know exactly how many times I grabbed a flashlight, made my way out of bed and the cabin to scan the area only to see that *Willow* had not moved. I did manage to train myself to avoid stubbing my toes on the bottom of the oval opening and to avoid the bolts that had scalped my head previously. I had difficulty gaining my bearing as *Willow* had shifted and the scenery had changed slightly.

Had we drifted closer? It was difficult to say. I figured that even if we had, we were still far enough away from any danger. Sleep deprived, I slipped in and out of consciousness. Unsure whether I was dreaming, somewhere between the hours of 3:00 a.m. and 5:00 a.m., I dreamed that I was on the boat trying desperately to sleep and my brother was there behind the wheel, steering. Somehow, he knew I couldn't sleep, that I was fighting it. He stuck his head inside the cabin and looked me in the eye like he knew I was suffering and said,

"Go to sleep brother, I got this."

A feeling of trust engulfed me. Just like that, I slept until dawn. But morning came too soon.

***

DAY THREE

Still miserably sore, I awoke in the early darkness. The converter display bathed the cabin in a blue hue. I reached over my head and turned the round, 120-volt fan off, then laid over on my back and gazed up at the dark sky through the open hatch above me. Silence and utter calm filled me.

"*Willow* is not even rocking. It's as if she still slumbers," I thought.

The river slept too. I noticed the absence of lapping water against her, a far cry from the scene last night. I rubbed my eyes as I stretched, pointing my toes as far as possible, relaxed, then sighed.

It's peaceful, different. If I were at home, I would simply roll over and go back to sleep. I could also do that here on *Willow*. But for the first time for as long as I could remember, I wanted to get up!

I started laughing as I reached up and grabbed the open hatch to help me to scooch myself down to the bottom of the bed. "To scoot down" implies control, ease—like you know what you're doing. "Scooching" is far less elegant. It was painful going. My stomach and leg started to cramp up.

"Jeez."

I just wanted to get out of bed!

When I finally flopped semi-down from the bed, I made my way towards the main hatch. Not picking my foot up high enough, I smacked my toes on part of the oval doorway and almost found my nose buried in the floor. Luckily, as I stumbled forward, my hands found their way to keep me from crashing completely onto the floor.

It's a tight squeeze down there for me, so I grasped what I could to help me up and continued toward the hatch. I hit the saloon doors with the palm of my hand, and they flung open with a bang. I reached a hand up and slid the cover back with another violent bang.

What a way to enter a new day. I stepped out of the hatch and threw my hands up like a Super Bowl ref calling the winning field goal.

"It's good!"

I stood, hands outstretched, laughing out loud. Shaking my head, I smiled and plucked the light from the boom, as if to remove the last Christmas ornament from the tree. Unplugging it, I stowed the light in its rightful place inside the cabin, just next to the rum where it could be easily found again in the evening.

I took a seat, poured a glass of water from the cooler and drank a refreshing deep drink. Evidently, I was getting dehydrated, for soon I had filled another. I drank slower this time. I figured the stomach ache I felt a short time later might have been the result of drinking too much water in such a short time.

I felt like a new witness to the sunrise as it climbed its way up out of the trees. The slight line of mist along the tree line made the scene look rehearsed...too perfect like a Photoshopped picture. A truck appeared; its lights moving along an unseen road that brought me out from within the framework, but the picture remained wondrous.

Unlike a house planted on solid ground, waking up on a boat feels good and inspires a sense of adventure. At home, everything is stable, the same thing day after day. But, like any other vessel, on *Willow* things change and those changes make an immediate impact on your day.

Spring a leak? Call a plumber?

Nope, you have to handle it immediately and by yourself. You must either make sure you fix it right the first time or fix it so it will get you to a destination where you can get someone else to do it properly. Otherwise, you may lose your floating home. Sounds like a lot of pressure, huh? It may feel like it while you're doing it, but the fix is often simpler than you think. You know, like pulling in and fixing your motor when it falls overboard.

I was grateful to wake up on *Willow* even though I awoke needing a nap. But I quickly found myself looking forward to getting the engine started and being on our way. With renewed determination, I removed the cover of the outboard motor and located the small brass screw. Once I saw it, it was obvious. Simple. I like that.

Loosening the screw only one turn, I began pumping the bulb in the gas line. I watched the milky water, drop by drop, fall from the bottom of the screw. After about ten minutes, I tightened up the screw and pushed the start button, but the motor locked up again. I painstakingly removed the spark plugs with one hand, careful to avoid dropping them in the water. My other hand cupped nervously underneath it, ready to catch a spark plug if it fell.

Once I had removed them, I loosened the brass screw, pumped a few times on the fuel bulb and watched the drops change color as they fell. I tightened up the brass screw once again and pressed start. The little motor turned fast as there were no spark plugs for compression. Gas fumes overwhelmed me. I carefully put the spark plugs and wires back in place and filled my cup with cold water from the igloo cooler.

Feeling a bit nauseous, I drank water while I waited for the fumes to dissipate. I figured the nausea was a result of the fact that I hadn't eaten very much. I shrugged it off, primed the fuel bulb, and I pushed the start button.

"Come on baby, start," I spoke to her.

The engine coughed once. My heart leapt into my throat. I knew she was going to start! A short thirty minutes of loosening the brass screw and priming the fuel bulb and she'd sprung to life. The little engine revved so high, I thought she was going to explode. I shut her down, waited a few minutes and pushed the start button.

"Come on baby," I chided her again.

She started right up, purring like a kitten.

"Yes, yes! Thank you, thank you, thank you!"

In my excitement I jumped up and headed forward along the side to pull up the anchor. Pulling the boat towards the anchor was slow going and difficult, so I thought about going back to put the motor in gear to speed up the process. In the end, I decided I could use the exercise. I needed to be in better shape if I expected to be able to repeatedly take up the anchor. The anchor line slacked as the boat bobbed down and I held the line tight as the boat bobbed back up until I was positioned directly over the anchor.

Pulling hard as the boat drifted over the anchor, I felt it let loose from the bottom. I pulled the anchor up, shaking it as best as I could to clear the mud off, then stored it and line in the locker. I headed back along the side of the boat, being careful not to stumble or fall overboard.

With the engine purring, I put her in gear, gave it a little twist and off we went. I noticed the motor bracket twisted slightly, but it didn't twist back. So, instead of the motor resting in the 12 o'clock position, it was more like 12:03, a barely noticeable difference.

"As long as she's moving, leave it alone," I said.

I looked back, shook my head and laughed.

"Third day out and I can still see where I started," I thought.

"Time to get moving."

I eased the throttle to 3/4 speed, careful not to twist the bracket with a quick acceleration, and set course away from

New Bern, North Carolina. A sense of pride coursed through me. I stood a bit taller behind the wheel.

Willow moved slowly. I could have kept up with her at a jog, but truth be told I can't jog for any distance. At least the motor wasn't cavitating.

The pristine, sunny and hot day with its slight breeze made me glad to be moving as I passed what I could only assume was Oriental, North Carolina. With such a long way to go, I realized how far behind schedule I'd become. I looked back and chuckled. Day three and I could *still* see where I started. The going was easy. I enjoyed the experience of motoring and watching the world go by. Some of the houses were beautiful, quite large with well-kept lawns and swimming pools. Others were just small cabins with little fishing piers, humble and quaint. I kept looking up to the top of the mast at the wind indicator, hoping for a change in direction but as for now I faced a headwind.

A slight headache gnawed behind my right eye, a tell-tale sign of the migraine that would soon come. I slipped down into the cabin in a fruitless search of my bag. I came to the painful realization that I had left my migraine shots behind. My migraines can last from a day to a week.

"I'm going to have to tough this one out," I thought.

I sighed and returned to the deck. I knew the smell of the sea and longed to taste the salt spray and feel it on my skin as I basked in the sun, wind and the waves.

I hadn't made it to the sea yet, still motoring through the brackish water. Its smell is different from the sea. It's the scent of old life; a musty blended combination of dirt mingled with the subtle smell of the brackish water, decaying marshland, and the life of the marsh.

I stood just in front of the opening to the cabin, my head resting on my smart hand, and my other on *Willow's* steering wheel. Relaxed and smiling, I couldn't stop grinning—like the Cheshire cat. It's the sort of grin that hurts your face. I'm not sure how long I stood there like that, but it felt like a forever moment packed into five minutes of complete solace and tranquility.

Motoring at a slight southeast course, I finally reached an area where I could turn her in a northerly direction. For the first time I raised the mainsail and the wind instantly filled the sail. For hours we moved along at quite a clip. Both motor and sail pushed her along. I peeked in on my stowaway. She awoke and was watching everything but still nestled in the protection of the celery under the clear plastic canopy.

By that time, I knew I was in trouble for my migraine was becoming intense. I would not be able to stay at the wheel for long. I went into the cabin in search of the autopilot. Locating it, I was able to quickly put it in use. The simple 4-button controller's steering arm moved in and out to correct the course. A small bolt at the end of the shaft connected to the old steering tiller. After making a few wide arches this way and tinkering, I finally got the hang of it. If I had been driving a car, I'm certain I would have been pulled over and given a sobriety test.

Once the autopilot became operational, I sat behind the wheel, head in my hands with the migraine painfully in full swing. I thought of my mom and dad and I replayed parts of the last three months of my Dad being in ICU. We'd almost lost him. At the time, I'd flown to their home in Maryland from mine in Texas and my sister had driven up from Florida, fearful that it was goodbye.

Once my dad was able to talk, we reminisced about the time my Dad, my brother and I went to Nags Head, North Carolina when I was in my mid-twenties. We had had such a great time. We finished that trip with the best of intentions to make the trip once a year, but it never happened again. We let life's distractions get in the way.

I'm sure that's a fairly common thing that happens to a lot of people. And it's crap. Distractions are the excuses we tell even ourselves when we know they are lies. I think it's hard to recognize your true self because there's a tendency to use less painful words to describe your behavior or to place the blame somewhere other than at your own feet. If the words we use define our character or our persona are full of excuses, they become our reasoning.

I was self-centered, lazy, and didn't care enough; more involved in my own life, my own wants and needs. Hard truth. Now I'm tired of excuses. Therefore, I have *Willow*. No more excuses. I wish to *experience* the rest of my time on earth not just live it. I can work myself into an early grave, or I can live. I'm hopeful that some of my family will enjoy *Willow* with me in the process.

About an hour before dark, motor-sailing up through the Pamlico Sound, I could see the clouds building up behind me. Hot on my heels the dark clouds rolled in, pushing *Willow*. I realized we could not outrun the storm. Lightning flashed in the distance. I glanced up at the huge lightning rod to which the sail is attached and chuckled to myself.

The migraine nearly at its peak, I sailed alongside a long, saltgrass island about an hour before dark. I could see the ferry that Yan had warned me about.

Unconcerned, I dropped the sail and motor taking a hard left before the ferry into a small cove etched behind the island. Just before the ferry landing, I tucked *Willow* into the cove. I could see the waves breaking over small gaps in the land as I dropped anchor.

"Perfect spot if I do say so myself," I thought.

The friend behind my eye continued to dig away with his red, hot icepick. I sat on the front deck waiting for the anchor rope to play out. My head in my hands, I felt the rain begin to hit my head and back, shocking cold at first. I tilted my head back eyes closed, face to the sky wanting the raindrops to find my eye and magically remove the pain. A few drops hit the mark and for a brief second the pain lessened to absorb this new feeling but returned just as strong as it had been.

When enough anchor line had played out, I pulled on the line and hoped the anchor would set as it caused *Willow* to straighten towards the reef. I made a figure eight with the anchor line around the cleat as the rain began to pour. I laid back and let the freezing cold rain wash over me, each drop like the small sting of a honey bee. I lay there, trying to keep the rain out of my nose and ears by covering my face with my hands, and hoping that the sudden change of body temperature would shock the migraine into submission.

I rolled over onto my stomach and cupped my face in my hands. The wind came in bursts driving the rain sideways and quickly filling my ear.

Lightning flashed.

One, one thousand.

Two, one thousand.

Three, one thousand.

Four, one thousand.

Five, one thousand.

Six, one BOOM!

Every muscle in my body jumped. WHOOO!

The migraine remained. I thought that if I could get my body shivering cold it might make it go away. So, I lay there, face down on the front deck, with a migraine in full swing in the cold wind and pouring rain as *Willow* bucked like a bronco and lightning bore down. I laughed and cried, unsure about what I was doing. It's kinda funny what you think about at times.

Bless all those who have never had a migraine. I'm happy for them, truly. But I have to be honest. Whenever someone tells me they've never had a migraine, especially when I'm in the throes of an intense one, I want to throat punch them.

I thought of the times I'd go to the emergency room and they would keep my room dark and cold, giving me up to seven shots to tone down the pain (which never worked). That was the case until I tried a drug called Imitrex which gave me relief and, in a sense, saved my life.

So, what the hell made me think this would work?

Half laughing and half crying, I got on my hands and knees and crawled to grasp the handrail to make my way back towards the cabin. My body started to tremble due to the loss of body heat. A bright flash of lightning mixed with the electric crackle in the air. BOOM!

No time to count. Close, too close. Trembling with numb hands I used trying to steady myself, I opened the cabin door. Sliding the hatch back, I just stepped forward as a bright flash, crackle and a sonic BOOM cause me to leap the rest of my body into the cabin all at once. WHOO! I thought it had me!

I slammed the hatch shut and pulled the saloon doors closed. Shivering, I made my way to the bed and I stripped naked dropping my clothes on the floor. I climbed into the bed and nestled into the covers. It was a good thirty minutes before the trembling eased, but the relentless migraine had taken a strong hold and still remained. There I laid, still a bit shaky but warming up. I pushed the palm of my hand onto my right eye and held on with my other hand as *Willow* pitched about while the storm raged.

Somehow, some time during the night, I fell into a fitful sleep, awakened by the constant pain of the migraine and the fear of dragging anchor or drifting aground. The cabin began to get hot, so I opened the hatch right above me and let the rain in to cool me off. It was like a game named hot or cold. The rain would cool me down and I would doze off until I would shiver from the cold. I would wake up enough to close the hatch, only to fall back asleep. To later wake up sweating to open up the hatch again. It was a miserable night.

***

DAY FOUR

THERE ARE ONLY TWO GREAT TRAGEDIES IN LIFE:
ONE IS NOT GETTING WHAT YOU WANT
AND THE OTHER IS GETTING IT.
OSCAR WILDE

The storm raged until early morning, but I woke to the sounds of the tranquil water lapping at *Willow's* side, still wet from opening the hatch during the night. I stretched as far as I could then popped open the hatch just above me. The sounds of the waves gentle on the shore of the narrow island filled the cabin. The sun had just started its peek over the horizon. I rubbed my eyes then made my way out of the bed and through the cabin. I smacked open the doors and slid back the hatch, stepping out like I owned the world.

To my surprise, not twenty yards away were two people in a small boat fishing by the shoreline. Still naked, I was surprised and kind of embarrassed. I had not heard them pull up. We awkwardly waved at each other and went about our business. The first thing I did was to go back in the cabin and get my shorts on. They fished while I cooked eggs and cheese as the sun made its debut. I ate breakfast directly out of the pan. No need for formalities. I pushed on the foot pump to wash the utensils. I had other plans for the pan. Utensils stowed away, I started the engine and let it warm up as I made my way to the bow to pull up the anchor.

After stowing the anchor, I scurried back and peeked in on the stowaway. She had moved deeper into the celery for protection and appeared to be sleeping. I'm sure she had had a rough night as well. My migraine, its claws buried deep behind my eye had not relented.

"It's going to be a long day," I thought.

I pulled out the nautical chart.

"Swanquarter National Wildlife Refuge. That's about where I'm at. Just south behind the elongated island."

Looking at the chart it appeared I'd have a bit of open water to get through before I could get into the intracoastal.

"Fine by me," I thought as I steered clear of the ferry's path.

"I'm in no condition to navigate today."

So, I prepared the autopilot, and motored *Willow* out of the cove and into the Pamlico Sound. I set course with the autopilot. I tied a rope to the frying pan handle and tossed it over the side and smiled.

"Autowash."

"Fun."

I pulled out the cushions that lay on the long bench seat to either side, put them both on one side and made myself as comfortable as possible. I brought a kitchen timer for just such an occasion. I wound it up to fifteen minutes and set myself in for a nap in an effort to sleep away the migraine. I constantly poked my head up and looked forward for boats, land, or anything else I might run into.

I moved the celery and its occupant into the shade. Try as I could to protect my feet, the sun always found them and began to roast them, so I moved to the floor of the cockpit. That was okay for a few minutes, but it soon became terribly hot. I could smell the fumes from the five gas tanks. That odor combined with the stifling heat made me nauseous. Bad idea. Also, my feet became tenderer by the minute as I considered the idea of sunburn on the bottom of my feet.

The timer went off and startled me. The first fifteen minutes hadn't gone so well. I stepped into the cabin. Nope, too hot. And it would take more effort than I was willing to give to keep getting in and out of the cabin. I stared at the boom above the top deck. I covered it with a cloth tent to create a small shady space that I hoped to fit under. I slid the hatch and the saloon doors closed and made my way up under the little boom tent. Stretching out under the boom wasn't bad at all. Best decision yet!

The slight breeze felt just right yet the sun seemingly searched for my feet as if we were playing hide and seek. I constantly moved them out of the sunlight. Looking to the horizon I made sure the coast was clear, twisted the dial to the fifteen-minute mark and closed my eyes. I never really slept because of the migraine, and because *Willow* was on the move. I was apprehensive about the alarm. Why? I have no idea.

There was a spot on the map I was curious about. It was an off-limits zone. I knew when we were coming close to it because a two-unit helicopter patrol took long sweeps around the area then focused on *Willow* for about fifteen minutes, hovering and staring at us. It felt kind of awkward, like an uneasy silence in a room filled with people waiting for a reaction about some remark someone shouldn't have said. So, I rolled over, looked around, gave the timer a little twist and closed my eyes. Moments later I heard the choppers pulling away.

It's a strange sensation, closing your eyes, trying to sleep off a migraine while the vessel you're lying on is plowing through the water with a blind pilot that only knows to go forward, regardless of what lies in its path.

The hours rolled by fifteen minutes at a time. My main focus during this part of my trek was to keep my body parts out of direct sunlight. While awake this was no problem, but once I would fall asleep, and a hand or a foot would slide into the sunlight. The blasting heat would wake me within a minute, and I'd adjust again.

This dance of the day went like this: "Ring," the alarm goes off. I'd look around, see something in the distance, get up and man the wheel until it passed. Then I'd lay back down, twist the alarm, close my eyes, and start to fall asleep until…

"My foot feels like it's on fire!"

I'd adjust position, glance at the timer, five minutes more. Ding! Look around and lay back down. Twist the timer. Here we go doe-see-doe…

Hours later, the migraine ebbed begrudgingly away, giving way to sweet relief; to be out from under that pain was most welcome. In its absence I felt renewed in every way.

Even at midday, I knew I had many hours before the sun set for the evening. I climbed down from under the boom and opened the cabin to review the nautical chart. I estimated we were approaching the northern portion of the Pamlico Sound, and soon we would be entering the Intracoastal Waterway.

Getting excited, I hauled in the "clean" frying pan, rinsed, dried and put it away. I checked on my stowaway. She stared at me from the back of the bag. I really couldn't imagine what she was thinking.

When I grabbed a big swig of water from the cooler, I noticed that the weathervane showed the wind blowing from the four o'clock position. Time to raise the mainsail!

I jumped up onto the cabin roof, my feet oddly tender, removed the cloth tent, loosened the halyard from its hold, attached it to the mainsail, and removed the bungees holding the sail as I made my way to the cockpit. Once there, I pulled the mainsail line as far as I could, raising the mainsail in the process. Wrapping the line twice around the wench, I grabbed the handle and slapped it into place.

Yan's words came to me. "Always slap the handle down hard to insure it gets set. You never want to lose one. And keep tension while cranking on the wench 'cause if it eats the line, you'll have to cut it. There's no other way to get it out once it's in there."

"And," he said, "You don't ever want to do that. It's a two-speed crank. You can use it like a ratchet to tighten it.

Two turns on the crank until the end, then two turns around the cleat and you're all set."

Willow moved at a good clip, I turned the motor off and tilted it out of the water. The air quieted around me except for the wind and the sounds of the bow slicing through the water. I watched the small wake behind the hulls. They each had their own. Another sailboat running parallel in the distance seemed to be pulling away. Suddenly I was losing an imaginary race!

I had two hulls and he had one, but we were comparable, about the same size. On the other hand, he had two sails up and I only had one. It was the jib I lacked. A bit apprehensive, I made my way to the bow. I had never raised a jib before, so I wasn't too sure how to go about it. I first looked ahead to insure our path was still clear. Then I tried to figure out how to raise it. I first pulled on the line bringing out the sail. As it flopped crazily around, I knew I must be doing something wrong.

"Unfurl the jib. Yes, that even sounds right."

I glanced around and noticed a pole in a holding slot on the top of the cabin. Jib pole!

"Okay, okay. Thank you, thank you thank you," I thought to myself.

I loosened the line and the jib rolled back up. Working the jib pole out of its hold, I held it in various positions but didn't have much of a clue. Then I remembered one of the movies I had watched where the jib was oddly held out by a pole that extended horizontally from the near bottom of the mast.

I surveyed the base of the mast. About three feet from the base was a very large metal eye. I clipped one end of the pole and looked out at the other end. Boom. There it was. Whether I had it right or wrong, I didn't care. It worked, so it was right at the time. I clipped the other end to the eyelet where the two lines attach, then I went to the cockpit to pull on the line. It took me several attempts to adjust the pole, but I finally succeeded, the jib filled with the wind and *Willow* increased her speed.

I loved the experience of moving along, silently slicing through the water. She sailed a bit slower than the waves, so every three to five minutes we slid down a wave and were picked up again into the next set of waves. It was a blast!

I picked up my headset and played a few songs, singing at the top of my lungs. I dropped my drawers and sailed buck naked until parts of me started to burn. I would drop the bucket with the rope on it over the side, haul it in, and dump it on my head to keep cool. Near the end of the Pamlico Sound the wind died down so I had to start the motor, so I motor-sailed into the entrance of the intracoastal, very proud of myself and excited.

The entrance made a winding right turn and I navigated the turn excellently, but to my surprise ahead I saw a shallow dead end. I was not in the intracoastal at all. Upon rounding the corner, I knew I was in trouble. I might have had thirty feet to turn around. I immediately released the mainsail and jib and cranked the wheel hard to come about. But the wheel broke free and just spun so I had no steering and was headed straight for land.

"Don't ever ground her. She's fourteen thousand pounds," Yan's words spoke to me again.

I sprinted back to the engine and turned her sideways to steer *Willow* away from the land, but the little engine would have none of it and it shut down.

"Crap!"

No steering, no motor, no nothing, but *Willow* had turned to where the sail filled with air and she started sailing directly to the shoreline. Panic stricken, I launched myself towards the bow, ripped the anchor and chain from its locker and sprinted towards the back of the boat, slinging the anchor as high and as far as I could. My shoulder screaming in protest.

Rushing back towards the bow I pulled in the slack. I stomped on the anchor line to get it as low as possible for a quick set on the bottom.

It seemed to be working, I felt the line tighten hard. I lashed the anchor line around the front left cleat and pulled hard, trying to keep *Willow* from running aground. About ten feet from shore she stopped and began a lazy turn to the port side. Pulling with all I had, fighting the sail, I was determined not to let her run aground. Hand over hand, I swung *Willow* around and when she was out of danger, I tied off the anchor line and proceeded to drop the mainsail and lash it to the boom. I pulled her in closer to the anchor and threw it out one more time for good measure. No time, the depth finder read zero...as in no more room.

This all happened so fast that I had not noticed the two people fishing not twenty yards away from *Willow*. Their jaws slacked as they stared at the madman on the sailboat. I threw up a quick wave hello but received no response. They just stared at like we were from another planet.

My only thought was, "Get me outta here."

I pushed the start button on the motor.

Click.

Again.

Click.

But they were small clicks. Okay. Okay.

Next up: steering!

I turned the boat's wheel to the left then to the right, but it just spun freely. I checked the steering line, but it was not slacked, so it wasn't a broken steering line. I went into the cabin and took apart the box behind the wheel. All looked good. Going back to the wheel, I popped off the round block of wood that covered the shaft. I found an adjustable wrench to fit the nut and backed the nut off. The problem became apparent once I had pulled the steering wheel. Yan had used a

3/4 threaded rod and had torqued it down to hold it in place. I had just overpowered it in my haste.

Laughing, I thought, "no problem at all!"

I knew just what to do. While working on the engine I had become privy to all the tools aboard and I directly recalled seeing a large, new pair of vise grips. More importantly, I knew exactly where they were. I slipped into the cabin and reappeared in a moment already adjusting them to fit tightly around the shaft. They would not be coming off.

"Vise grips," I said, "What's in your box?"

My own commercial!

Aye, and there I was...four days out at sea. Alone, fightin' the storm, struggling to keep her on course, putting all I had into the wheel. Pushing her hard when all of a sudden, a loud snap pierced the silence as the wheel broke free and the good ship *Willow* floundered.

She turned her own way, aside the lull between the twenty-foot waves. Then all hell broke loose as I lunged for the cabin door. Hanging on for dear life, my hand grasped the tool that could fix what no other can.

I charged back towards the helm where the wheel itself had abandoned ship. And there, with all my strength, I fastened the vice grips onto to the shaft and steered the vessel out of harm's way.

The sea seemed less formidable. The clouds parted letting the sun shine down, the sea drew calm and the dolphins played, and birds chirped. What a glorious day it turned out to be! All because I keep a pair of all-original, American made vice grips in my tool box.

What's in your box?

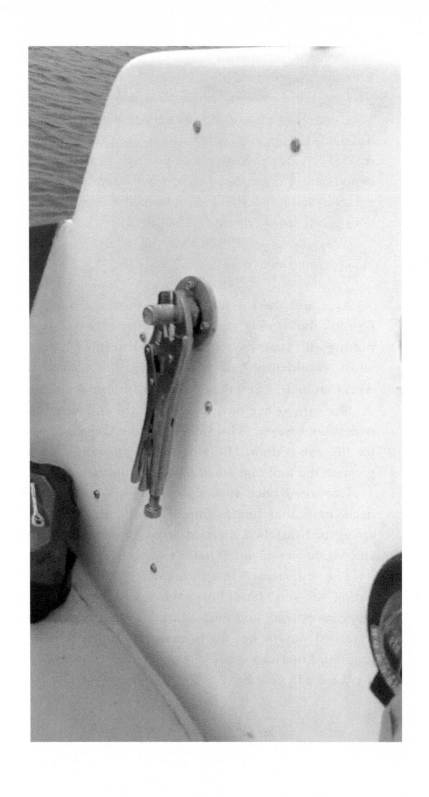

Okay, that might be a bit much. But I did skit that out right then and there. I glanced over my shoulder and the two men on the shore still stared open-mouthed like cardboard cut-out props until one reached down, picked up a beer, drank deep and set it back down. His eyes never left me.

Laughing at my predicament, I set about taking off the engine cover. Looking at the starter I saw the gear stuck in the "up" position, having no travel space. Therefore, it would just click. I manually wound the gear down the shaft and pushed the button. The gear slammed home properly, and she sprang to life. Another catastrophic moment avoided.

I had not felt this alive in quite some time. I left the little motor run as I headed towards the bow, hauled up the anchor, shook it off and rushed to store it in its locker. Heading back, I took a last look at the fishermen, smiled as big as I could and threw out my best Forrest Gump wave. They simply looked at each other then back at the crazy sailor who obviously didn't know what he was doing.

Smiling to myself, I put the little motor in gear, turned it sharply to the left, gave her some throttle and watched gratefully as she turned. I turned back toward the shoreline, and with a flourish, threw my hand outward with a sweep gesturing to *Willow*, placed the other on my stomach and bowed to the audience of two as we departed the quaint little cove.

Bound for the proper entrance to the Intracoastal Waterway, we traversed the mere five hundred yards ahead and continued our journey. Unmistakable, I knew that I had reached the ICW when I saw a forty-foot trawler go into it. I made a large sweeping pass around the land and soon found myself navigating through. I first made a sweep to the right then a hairpin turn to the left.

I could look back to the marsh and see parts of houses, overturned boats, trucks, and campers. All rested in random places in awkward positions, some rusted with age, others of more recent demise, but all reminded that tranquility is passing.

I reckon it's like that at any seaside considering the possibility of devastation from high water and storms. Nevertheless, we remain drawn to the sea despite the possible dangers. Its power, seemingly spiritual can make us feel differently than we do in our everyday lives. It gives to us a difference of experience, an emotional support, or a friend that will always be. We can shout and scream at it, throw rocks at it and it will take it and still be there waiting for more. We can play in it, jump in, enjoy it. We can also just sit and absorb all it has to give and admire its natural beauty. It is forever. We are not.

While I tooled slowly up the Intracoastal, I had time to retrieve the map and lay it across the cabin top. Found my location. I made note of the miles I had traveled from the place where I had started to my current location. At my present speed, just motoring up to the Potomac would take a week.

"Just don't think about it, do it," I admonished myself.

I started looking for a place to pull over to scrape the bottom. Ironically, within thirty minutes I motored past an Alligator Refuge sign.

"Don't think about them."

Lord have mercy. My heart sank. Motoring up another thirty minutes or so, I came upon a small park with a wide boat ramp. If Yan could do the scraping, so could I.

"Just don't think about them."

I made my way into the boat ramp and tied off as far back from the ramp as I could. People picnicking in the park enjoyed the day. I scouted the area and water for alligators (just in case.)

With my mind made up, I began searching for the scrapers. I had lost a medium-sized heavy scraper along with a 10mm socket when I was trying to save the engine. I did find a two-foot scraper and the small one my brother had given me "just in case." I gathered gloves and a bit of Paracord that I used to tie a scraper to each hand. I donned my life jacket and ran the straps up between my legs for extra support. I erected the ladder, hooked it to the transom and slowly made my way into the dark, lukewarm water, scrapers hanging from each hand.

I rubbed my gloved hands across the hull, feeling the inch-thick growth. It hadn't looked that bad from up on the boat. I sighed and put the big blade to it. Having the life jacket with the straps running through my legs assisted in the stability. Almost in a seated position, my legs and male parts dangled (which made me a bit nervous.) My mind chattered.

"Don't think about them."

"Kibbles and Bits, Kibbles and Bits."

"Don't think about them."

"Yan did it, you can do it!"

"Kibbles and Bits."

"Stop!"

"Get to scraping."

Wasting no time, I scraped in a controlled panic. The barnacles came off like an old shag carpet that had never been cleaned or vacuumed. I had let go of the two-foot scraper to adjust my life jacket. Apparently, I had severed the paracord while I was scraping. It disappeared. I tiptoed all around the bottom. I could not locate it but gave up on the search quickly because...well, I didn't like my feet being that far from me.

"Don't think about them."

"Kibbles and Bits and Pieces."

"Stop!"

I resigned myself to use the small four-inch putty knife that my brother had given me and scraped like a mad man. I thought that the quicker I got done, the faster I could get my own kibbles and bits out of the water.

In the water under the cockpit, between the hulls, I applied a bit of elbow grease and scraped away on the inside of the port hull. It started to come along nicely. Every now and then I would scrape at too close of an angle and my glove would get shredded by the barnacles. In short order, my knuckles were bleeding. I know that sharks can smell a single drop of blood miles away.

"What about alligators?" I wondered.

"Never mind. I don't want to know."

My hands started scraping faster. I reached the port rudder having no clue it could be pulled up! It was terribly heavy, even after I scraped it. I could only hold it up for a moment as my toes sunk deeper into the bottom. It was a bit tricky getting all the growth of the smaller areas, but I managed. Heavily sweating, I wished I had brought some water to drink. I considered taking a break to get a drink, but I knew if I got out, I probably wouldn't get back in.

"Get 'er done. Just get her done!"

Working my way to the outside of the port hull, scraping became much easier as I pushed off the bulkhead with my feet and free hand. Soon I had a system; working the scraper with both hands, peeling off at least a foot-long section at a time. I had finally come around the bow of the stern hull with only a third left to finish.

A young boy and his father walked down to the small pier not twenty yards in front of *Willow*. I could hear as the boy plead with his father to go swimming.

"NO, there are alligators in that water," the father said emphatically.

Just when I had slacked up on the scraping, their interaction provided me with renewed energy as if the president of the company had just walked into the boardroom and I needed to impress him to get that promotion. About halfway down the inside of the port hull, I just kinda hovered in my life jacket when something big brushed up against my left leg.

I'm not sure what kind of noise I made. To be honest it was something between a girl's scream and an owl's screech followed by, "No, no, no," and a variety of single syllable words. Simultaneously, I slammed my feet to the bottom which caused my head to smack the underside of the cabin which damn near knocked me out. I grabbed my kibbles and bits and held them until I felt it was safe.

Everyone within earshot or view of me froze and stared at me, like, "Alligator?"

It wasn't one of my proudest moments. Breathing hard, sweating more, I rationalized quickly that whatever it was, was big but it was smooth. I hadn't felt any feet or claws. Best of all, I wasn't fighting for my life.

"Breathe. Now back to work."

I'm surprised that I didn't drop the scraper. Then I realized that the smart hand held it like a knife, which turned it into the only weapon I had.

"Good boy, now let's get back to scraping."

Once I completed the port hull, I could see a large difference in the water line between it and the starboard hull. It appeared to have lifted at least four inches which gave me an idea how much those barnacles must have weighed. Anxious to complete the task, I was a bit nervous about it too.

"Don't think about them. Just get to work."

After another hour of scraping, I threw the scraper up into the cockpit and made my way to the ladder. Worn out and not wanting to climb up, I thought, "Heck, I'll walk up the boat ramp. Sure thing."

People were all over the place as I started walking up the boat ramp. The people closest who saw me stopped and motioned to their friends and they stopped and stared at me. Slightly annoyed, I thought, "What? Have you never seen anyone walking up a boat ramp? Jeez. Give me a break!"

Completely out of the water when I finally looked down at myself, I realized why. I looked like I was a hairy Sasquatch, but I only have about eight chest hairs and those are white. I looked down further to my legs, bushy black hair.

"Okay. Dirt. No big deal."

I turned and went back, knee deep into the water and splashed myself off to rinse off the dirt. Bear in mind I need readers to see detail, like when I am reading. All rinsed off and happy to be alive, I made my way back to *Willow*, excited because she'd move a lot faster having shed the weight.

When I stepped aboard, I pulled the ladder and stowed it. I jumped into the cockpit, fired up the engine and casted off. I used the motor to steer, a made a hairpin tight U-turn. I eased out of the turn and noticed the entire bottom of the cockpit covered in moving black muck. I couldn't tell what it was without my glasses. I grabbed them and looked at the pile.

"Whoa, Holy, Jiminy Crickets, Whaaaaaat the Sam Hill?"

Willow narrowly missed the bulkhead on the other side, but I managed to turn the motor just in time as I tried to get my feet out of this huge pile of worms that kept falling out of my life jacket and shorts!

"Holy Good Gawd Almighty."

My stomach churned at the sight.

I steered *Willow* away from shore while I smashed the worms with my feet and removed my life jacket as more fell onto my feet and the deck.

Rapid fire thoughts plagued me. "And my shorts...oh Lord, I gotta get my shorts off!"

Too many people, and too many kids could see me!

"Oh, hell."

My gut reaction told me to rip my shorts off and jump in the water, but I couldn't do it with so many people and the chance of alligators about. Thinking fast, I threw the bucket with a rope attached, dragged it in, pulled open my shorts and dumped the water down my front.

"Oh my God."

"No, no, no, no, no, no!"

I threw the bucket again and again dumping water into my shorts, this time in the back.

"Oh Lord mercy, they are everywhere!"

I felt them every place imaginable. Ten, fifteen, twenty times I dumped the water, front, back, sides, shaking my shorts the entire time. They just keep pouring out like a live horror movie. I could feel them trying to attach themselves to the newly found home, me!

Finally, after about two hours of chucking the bucket and rinsing, I changed shorts and rinsed off the last of the little worms from myself and the deck. Months later when retelling the story, the hairs on my arms would stand straight up and I would still get that feeling in the pit of my stomach as I remember the feeling as the thousands of small worms tried to attach themselves to every part of my body.

Luckily, I had planned to stay the night at a small marina up ahead. There I would replenish my supplies of water, ice and fuel. If they had a shower, I'd be having two or three until I no longer felt those worms on me.

Cruising up the ICW, I was amazed and thrilled at how quickly *Willow* moved through the water, much faster than I had anticipated. Her speed had almost doubled.

"The rest of the trip should be a breeze," I thought.

Upon rounding a bend, I could see the small marina in the distance. As I approached about five hundred yards from the marina, the motor died and then the starter died. I pulled the cover to take a look. The gear that goes up and hits the flywheel was in its proper place, but no click from the starter.

"Okay, emergency pull cord. I know I saw it somewhere." After about fifteen minutes of dragging all the boxes out and rummaging through everything, I gave up. I grabbed a piece of rope, made a double knot on the end, wrapped it around the flywheel and pulled. What a pain the arse.

The motor, at least two feet away from the transom, made it challenging to get to. I wrapped the rope around it again, pulled it hard but I pulled it too high which caused the rope to release and slap me in the face. Keeping it low, I tried it again. The motor started, but the fingernail on my pinky finger caught the transom and bent backwards. I thought I'd broken my finger. Holding my hand in a tight fist to ease the pain, I put the motor in gear and rode slowly to the marina.

The tiny Coinjock Marina, a bulkhead of maybe five hundred feet had a few slips at the north end that looked to belong to the few houses there. I could see the faces of the people in the five hundred thousand-dollar, three story yachts as I passed by as I did a sharp U-turn and snuggled in between two bigger multi-million ones just for grins. I could almost hear them.

"If he hits us, who is going to pay damages?"

I knew instantly I would be asked to move to the end of the dock further away but I didn't mind. I chuckled because I gave them a bit of a scare. A man who watched me as he paced the dock approached.

"Ahoy Captain!" he spoke.

"He's talking to me!" I thought, shocked.

That was unexpected but appreciated. I knew that I did not warrant the title.

"If he only knew," I thought.

"Yes sir. How's it going?" I asked.

"Fine, fine. Good day to be on the water. What can I help you with?" he asked.

"Nothing really, I just need gas and ice, and oh, a place to shower if you have one. Is this your marina?" I inquired.

"No Cap, I'm the dock mate. Let's get you started with your gas. The ice is there in the store. Showers are there on the side of the restaurant. Will you be staying the night?" the dock mate asked.

"If you have room, it would be nice," I said.

"Yes sir," he said. "When you finish your business would you mind pulling to the north end of the dock please?" he continued.

"Will do!" I said, "And thank you!"

I had no idea that my feet were in such bad shape until I walked up on the deck towards the store. I felt every space between the boards and every crack and crevice in each board. My feet had been tenderized and become painfully raw which made me grateful for the store's smooth, cool, vinyl flooring.

The store didn't have much in the way of supplies. I wanted a deck brush to clean off the front where the anchor and chain had muddied the deck. I found the brush and metal pole sold separately.

"This might hurt a bit," I thought as I headed to the counter with my prize. I hung my head as I returned them to their resting place. The hundred twenty-dollar price hurt a bit too much.

"Whew, I'm living life wrong. A hundred and twenty bucks for a stick with a brush on the end. Holy moly!" I mumbled to myself.

To their credit, it was a nice set up, but I was afraid to ask the price of anything else. I had to have the gas and I wanted the ice. I returned to the cashier, she had that old salt look with tanned, slightly wrinkled skin, long white hair and hazel eyes. You could tell she was a knockout in her younger years as she still held her attractiveness. She sported a white tank top with the marina's logo on the front. Those were fifty dollars. (I had hoped they were around twenty, so I settled for a cup.)

"Is there a public shower?" I inquired.

"Yes, it's free if you're docking for the night. Do you plan on staying the night?" she asked.

"Yes ma'am, and I'm sure I smell as bad as I look, so I'll be looking forward to the shower."

"The shower is on this side of the restaurant," she said.

I paid for the night dockage, fuel, and three, twenty-pound bags of ice—a quick hundred and forty-eight dollars. I handed her a hundred and fifty. She returned my two dollars change, leaned in and said, "You do look better than you smell," as she winked and smiled.

Nodding her head back, she added, "There's a band tonight outside at the restaurant. You go have yourself a good night."

"Y-Yes ma'am, you too. Thank you."

I really didn't know what to say or feel. She really caught me off guard.

I walked gingerly back towards the waiting *Willow* carrying the bags of ice. Damn, my feet really hurt. I slung the ice aboard, laying them in the long bench behind the vice grip wheel. I climbed into the cockpit, grabbed the igloo cooler, removed the top, looked in and gagged.

There, floating in the water were the eight fresh pork patties I bought days ago, pale and ruined. I pulled the patties out as they fell apart which finally explained why I felt sick every time I drank water from it. Ugh! It made me ill just thinking about it. I scooped it all out, threw it in the trash, dumped the water and scrubbed it out.

"Hey Cap! Can I get you to go ahead to the end down there?" the deck hand called.

"Yes sir! Right away! Once I get the engine started, just cast off the lines and I'll head that way."

"I'll meet you to tie off."

"No need, I've got it, but thank you," I answered.

I admit I was embarrassed when I had to remove the motor cover and take four times wrapping the rope around the flywheel before it started. But once the motor started, he cast me off.

"You sure you don't want me to come up to tie you off?"

"No sir, I've got it. But thanks!"

"Okay Cap, you have a good night. There's showers on the south side of the restaurant."

"Great! I'm looking forward to it, thank you!"

Once out, I made an immediate U-turn and headed to the back forty of the bulkhead. I did another U-turn and eased up to the bulkhead like a pro, jumped onto the wooden deck and my feet quickly reminded me they were in pain.

After I tied off *Willow*, I decided to wash her down since she was dirty from bow to stern. A small, lighthouse-looking structure about four foot-high held the electrical connections for the power cords to the boats. Of course, there were no extension cord plugs. That was okay with me. I was after the water hose. I pulled plenty of hose to wash wherever I needed to and gave my girl a bath. I felt bad, for she looked hard-used with all the mud and muddy footprints forward and aft. I found a small scrub brush and down on all fours I scrubbed her down: the entire front deck sides, cabin, bench seats, cockpit, and I finished with the cooler. Half a bottle of dish soap and she was beautiful once again. I told her so and promised I would do my best to keep her that way.

I grabbed a clean pair of shorts, shirt, and put on my water shoes, grabbed a towel and my ditty bag and headed for the shower. Walking down the dock where all the magnificent, expensive yachts were parked in rows, I was genuinely amazed. The owners were dressed as elegantly as their yachts, and I totally get that. I was dressed as elegantly as mine too!

No one paid me any mind and I was glad for it. Walking past those well-heeled customers as they ate their evening meals, toasted with wine, beer, and cocktails, I felt less than them and I was relieved to find the hot, stagnant showers empty.

I hung my towel and clothes and turned on the shower, waiting for the water to warm as the air-conditioner labored hard. I popped open the cover and pulled out the two washable filters that were caked solid with dirt. I could almost hear the AC unit sigh with relief. I took the filters into the shower where it took about ten minutes to get them clean. I stuck them back in. It already felt better. They probably hadn't been cleaned since they were put in.

"My turn!" I thought.

I opened my bag, pulled out my toothbrush and toothpaste, but no soap.

"Oops. I'm not going all the way back for that."

I went to the sink and pumped the liquid soap into my hand, shoved it in my pocket, did the same to the other pocket, then all over my shorts, shirt, under arms and legs and made my way carefully back to the shower to scrub. Washing my shorts and shirt first, I rinsed, squeezed and hung them on the hook. After I shaved my face, I felt so clean, I just stood there under the shower for a while.

As I put up my things and dried off, I realized how hungry I was. Quickly putting on my clean shorts and shirt, I shot out the door. I walked completely through the area of tables where people were eating to set up against the tall, long, bar height table that ran the length of the wooden split rail fence. That separated the bulkhead dock from the patrons enjoying their dinner with a sign that read, "Boat Owners and Guests Only".

"What can I get for you?" the bartender asked.

"Your mussels as an appetizer."

"We have a homemade chips and salsa."

"I'll take that too, and your porterhouse steak."

"It's that all?"

"Oh, yes, and two margaritas, please!"

The band's lead singer had a voice that would make Stevie Nicks proud, and I told her so when I got the chance. She and her husband played great together. I sang along, out loud so she asked me to come up and do a song with her since I had also accompanied them with my air drumming.

I politely declined as I was thoroughly enjoying where I was. Just then, the mussels showed up with the two margaritas. Perfect timing. I demolished the mussels in two songs. The band was on their third set when the porterhouse steak and sweet potatoes arrived with two more margaritas. I was in heaven. The steak was excellent, and the drinks and the band rocked. It had shaped up to be a good night. Halfway through the porterhouse, I finally threw in the towel, asked for the check and a To Go box.

The band actually asked me to stay. We really were having that great a time, but I had to go. I needed to get some rest because tomorrow would be a long day. We said our goodbyes as I headed down the dock where only owners and their guests could tread.

As I made my way onto *Willow*, I put the leftover steak and potatoes in the cooler, pulling out the small block of cheese. The chips and salsa would not fit so I broke off some cheese and tried the chips.

"Not too bad," I thought.

I got a big glass of water from the igloo cooler.

"No upset stomach tonight! No more pork water for me!"

I turned on the inverter and the fan and laid down for the night in the hot, still air, grateful for the fan. Around 1:30 a.m. a loud shrill buzz, a hundred times louder than the annoying tone that reminds that you left your truck lights on, split the silence. It seemed to be coming from the yacht directly in front of me. I reckon it lasted for a good five minutes. I had just started to make my way out of the bed to find the source when it stopped.

I hollered, "Thank you!"

No reply. Nothing. They'd probably had more margaritas than me.

"No worries," I thought, "Good night."

Sometime later it happened again; the ear-splitting buzzer. I laid there, getting madder and madder until I couldn't stand it anymore and I got out of bed. Just as I slammed open the saloon doors and shoved the hatch back, the loud buzzing sound faded. At the same time my fan shut down. I realized that the horrible sound had been coming from my converter. I sat down in front of it and put on my glasses.

A normal reading, while it's not in use, is about 13.6 minimum input. I'd seen in the evenings at anchor the reading ranged between 11 and 12 input, but just then it read 7.6.

"Well, this means no fan in this heat for you tonight," I told myself.

I could see why Yan had said, "Never stay in a marina unless you have to."

All of the boats together block the breeze. If you're in a marina too long, you'll end up with mold and you'll have to run an AC unit just to be comfortable. That'll cost more too. I still wished I had air conditioning, but I saw his point and agreed with him. Still I complained about the heat as I laid down. With all the hatches open, sweating, I fell asleep.

A scratching noise on the top of the cabin near the open
hatch by my feet, similar to the sound of beach seagulls
landing on a car's roof, woke me.

I popped my head up and looked down at my feet. The fattest raccoon I have ever seen in my life was hanging from the hatch by one paw. As he swung around our eyes locked.

"OH, HELL NO!"

I swear he winked at me, then let go, falling to the floor.

"Holy crap!"

I pulled my feet up and scrambled around to get on all fours trying to see him. I had nowhere to go. Too fat to go any other way, I was a captive! Although there was plenty of light from the marina, I scrambled around but could not see him.

He wasn't down at the bottom of the bed where he had fallen. So, I sat there on all fours, quietly listening for any sound. Then I heard him again. He was opening my To Go box with the homemade chips and salsa. I banged on the side next to the table and I heard him jump down to the other side. I had to move quickly, he was going to run out of room fast and come back, so I had to get the doors open. Banging again on the side wall I jumped down and moved toward the saloon doors as fast as I could.

I grabbed the leftovers as I slapped open the saloon doors and stumbled out, bringing the leftovers with me. I jumped from *Willow* onto the wooden deck, as my feet seemed to scream in protest. I set the leftovers down on the dock and took a seat about ten yards down on a bench. Feet throbbing, I watched and waited. In seven minutes tops, he emerged from *Willow* onto the deck and made a beeline towards the chips and salsa, popped open the box and went to town.

I gingerly made my way down to the showers and stepped in to a nice cooling shower, shorts and all. Afterwards, I made my way back dripping wet.

The raccoon was nowhere around. The To Go box was in the grass. I threw what he'd left in the trash, boarded *Willow*, shut the saloon doors and crawled, soaking wet, into bed for a few hours of sleep to an orchestra of frogs and crickets. I imagined they had played their version of the "Mission Impossible" soundtrack for the raccoon.

***

DAY FIVE

CHARACTER IS GREATER THAN INTELLECT. A GREAT SOUL WILL BE STRONG TO LIVE AS WELL AS THINK.
RALPH WALDO EMERSON

I woke at daybreak, feeling surprisingly well, without the aftereffects of the tequila, thank goodness! I worked on the motor to get her going and she finally purred to life. I checked the map and counted seven bridges and one lock on the route. I'd never been through a lock before.

Looking forward to it I cast off the lines, slipped into a U-turn and motored away before other people were up and about. I hoped that after a few hours of running the motor with the solar panels that the battery would charge up. After a few hours it had only reached 9 volts. I had hoped for more, so I figured there was a drain on the battery somewhere. I turned off everything with the exception of the VHF radio— even the autopilot. I was getting plenty of practice with my newly installed vice grip steering wheel.

I checked in on my stowaway. Alas, she had jumped ship sometime overnight. I'm sure that wherever she disembarked, it felt like home to her. The frogs were especially loud. Maybe they had called to her.

Perched behind the wheel I ate my breakfast of porterhouse steak and potatoes, enjoying that the leftovers tasted even better cold. Cruising up the peaceful, narrow intracoastal, trees lined the waterway. Small cabins on stilts dotted the landscape.

A large yacht barreled down on me, so I moved to the side of the waterway to let it pass. The yacht never slowed. I was angry at first but then I could see why. At its speed, it barely left a wake. Had it slowed down, the wake would have been much choppier. I waved but it was not returned, maybe he was having a bad day.

I have known a few millionaires. They have had their ups and downs, but they seemed mostly down, still searching for something they could not yet identify. This took me back to a conversation I had with an elderly friend of mine named Lamar.

"If you would just focus, you would be a millionaire," he'd say.

What he failed to understand was that I had already been a millionaire, but I didn't care for the struggle and stress it took to maintain such a life. I was not happy. Don't get me wrong, I enjoyed driving a Jaguar and a Mercedes and living in a really nice house with a pool and jacuzzi. But when it came down to it, I had neglected those that I loved in trade for amassing a lot of money. Working 16-hour days, 7 days a week would take its toll on any relationship as it had dome with mine I had only myself to blame.

To be an elite, top dog is overrated. You know what's not overrated? Just being you, doing what your heart compels you to do. Like a lot of people, I've always wanted to be somebody other than who I was. But I've come to find out that everything that I thought I wasn't is everything that I am.

I took marine engine and boat building along with advanced auto mechanics while in high school because I didn't have the money to afford either a boat or car. And truthfully, I wasn't that good academically in high school. The trades that I learned set the foundation for me being able to work on all my vehicles until I started making enough money to pay someone else to do it.

I've reached a point in my life that I believe I'm living with my heart. You don't have to make a million dollars and if that's your goal, you're going to miss a lot of life's most precious moments which you'll probably regret at the end of your life. You'll spend all that time and effort while nobody else cares whether you are a millionaire or not. Why put yourself through all that? Just be happy. Time is running out.

I've worked in the air conditioning business for 35 years, and I enjoyed it for the most of that time because it made people happy. I enjoyed being their hero; that guy who would come out at 10pm and get them cool so they could sleep. I enjoyed it because it made me feel I was something more, even if it was just for a moment.

Now that work has become more and more difficult to do. Heart attacks and heat strokes have caused me to pause and reevaluate what I want to do and the person I want to be.

For instance, I've always wanted to be a rock star. Silly? Maybe. I wanted people to enjoy my singing even though I'm not that good and I've never sung in public. My little town of Sargent, Texas helped me do just that. I bought karaoke equipment and have had the best time being a local rock star. Yes, I know it's just karaoke but to me it means a lot. My friends make me feel like a star. It's all about perspective and what makes me happy.

I passed an old abandoned railroad bridge. I'd never seen such a thing. The portion of the bridge that extended over the water stuck straight up in the

air and looked to be at least a hundred feet high with mammoth wagon wheeled gears on each side, and a good size operator's cabin hanging onto one side.

"That would be a great weekend retreat," I thought to myself.

While passing by I had an eerie feeling that it might come crashing down. Heavily rusted, it looked like it could collapse at any minute.

Around lunch time I came upon the first swing bridge. It was similar to the one near my home in Sargent, Texas. Boats were already lined up waiting to go through. I stopped about a mile away, put her in neutral, went inside the cabin and emerged shortly with a delicious peanut butter and jelly sandwich. I poured a cup of ice-cold water and enjoyed drifting towards the other boats.

All power boats, I noticed one that had a bunch of kids who were playing *Old Time Rock and Roll* by Bob Seger. It reminded me of one day years back. At the time, Terri, the mother of my children and I had an 18-foot Cobia with the walkthrough windshield. She loved her some Bob Seger and I recall we blasted some good music too when we were out with our best friend Lisa and another guy. I can't remember his name anymore, but dummy here was driving the boat that day and damn near killed us all wave jumping. Of course, the engine died in the middle of it, but I had managed to get it started just before I stuck a landing on the beach. I got us out of that jam and slowed my roll. We spent the rest of the day getting toasted on beer and sun, but that was my youthful recklessness.

I cringe even today when I think of the close calls I've had. I'm lucky to still be around. We were all so young back then with no clue at all how our lives would turn out.

While daydreaming of those youthful indiscretions, I hadn't noticed that the bridge had opened and all of the boats had made it through except me. The bridge operator blasted its horn in protest of my delay. I quickly put the motor in gear and twisted the throttle. I watched in terror as the motor twisted up and only one of the clamps held the motor on.
I slowed down, but I continued heading towards the bridge. I loosened the clamp that was unattached, eased off the

throttle, put her in neutral, loosened the other clamp and slammed the motor back in place. Tightening up each clamp, I put her back in gear, slowly twisted the throttle and I waved to the bridge tender as I motored through.

Just a short distance ahead, I pulled to the side, dropped her in neutral and shut her down. I went to the bow, tossed the anchor, set it and went back to the motor. Damn my feet hurt! With determination, I thought, "I'm not having any more of that."

Upon inspecting the motor clamps and bracket, I realized how lucky I was that the motor had not come off much earlier. I couldn't really see it but when I had tightened both clamps, they were all the way in and had bottomed out. They *felt* tight but they were not. Snug yes. Tight no.

When I had originally moved the motor, a small, thin painted board shaped perfectly fit in that spot. I found where I had stashed it, loosened both motor brackets, slipped the piece of wood in place and tightened down hard on the motor mounts. She wasn't going anywhere.

I lashed a rope a few turns from the motor to the transom and tied it off just in case. I then pulled the motor cover and pull-started the motor. I headed up to the bow and pulled in the anchor, stowed it and climbed back into the cockpit. With the motor in gear we headed towards the locks.

On this breezy, overcast day perfect for sailing, I enjoyed watching people as I leisurely cruised by in my own private world. Another swing bridge, another town. I approached the locks. The sign read: "Life Jacket on When in the Locks."

Donning my life jacket, I glanced around as I pulled into the locks. I put her in neutral and moved to the left side. I grabbed the anchor line, ran it through the front port side cleat on the boat, up around the cleat atop the steel bulkhead, around the other cleat some twenty feet back, then down to the aft cleat on the boat. Without thinking through the process, I just tied the ones on the boat.

After about twenty minutes, the lock gates behind me moved out from the wall and met in the middle. I went into the cabin to pull out the map. I placed it on top of the cabin and stood in my usual spot in the entryway when I felt myself leaning towards the right.

"Weird," I thought.

I looked back and realized that the water was leaving the lock and the port side of the boat was tied off and being hung in place as the rest of the boat was being lowered. Things started sliding to starboard, the entire port side was out of the water! I scrambled to untie the aft line, but it was too tight. I jetted back to the cabin and grabbed the Swiss army knife my father had given me. Another few minutes and I was sure I would lose *Willow*.

As fast as I could I reached the rope and touched it with the knife, the rope snapped so abruptly I almost fell in the water. I was thankful that I had not tied to any of the cleats on the top of the steel bulkhead. At that point, the bulkhead was ten feet high and out of reach. Luckily, I only lost about three feet of anchor line. I steadied myself and looked around. A bit embarrassed, I imagined someone was getting a chuckle out of it. I saw no one, and if anyone in the control room saw, they didn't let on. I realized that I could have lost *Willow*. The lowering water would not have stopped. It could have been tragic. I'd put to use the lost, small section of anchor line to practice my new favorite knots. I walked up *Willow's* side and pulled in the slack anchor line, stowing it back in its locker.

A few moments later the northern gates of the lock opened. Looking up at the metal bulkhead, I estimated that it had dropped around twelve feet. Shaking my head at the near miss, I put her in gear and puttered slowly out of the lock. The destination sign in the lock showed two hundred miles to Baltimore. I figured Valley Lee was half the distance which in turn made me about three quarters of the way home.

Coming up next was Portsmouth, Virginia which had been my first duty station back in 1983, and then Norfolk and the Chesapeake Bay. I planned on staying by the old naval hospital for the nostalgia. The sights while motoring up the ICW made for a great experience.

As I neared Portsmouth, large Navy destroyers lined the water way. It was Sunday, so there were not too many people around. I came upon a tall bridge that had an open metal grate lane. I laughed hard when I heard the sound the cars made as they drove over it like huge bumble bees.

Some ships were in dry dock, others in the water. Most had enormous covers draped over them so you could not see certain parts of the ships. The sight made me feel small and insignificant yet proud at the same time for it would take several thousand beings like me to become the most significant power on the water—the U.S. Navy. I was proud to have been a part of that.

I could see the Waterside fair that sits across the waterway from the Portsmouth Naval Hospital. I knew I was getting close. Difficult at first to pick out, I saw my first duty station. I pulled around to the side of the loop where the Special Service building stood where I had met Teri. I tossed out the anchor and stood on the bow.

I recalled a looping path in the park where I once walked and later sat on one of the benches taking long drags from a cigarette as I looked at the Ferris wheel across the water. Unsure of my life at the time, I couldn't seem to get it right. Memories flooded my mind. I was reminded of friend's names that I had long since forgotten: P.J., Jack, Chief Blanchard, Bambi, Pete, Tommy Limley, Sacho, and many more.

Tears filled my eyes as I replayed moments from long ago. It seemed such a loss. Thirty-four years and I'd come full circle. I was not ready for the emotions this evoked, and they got the best of me. I'd practiced for years silencing the voice in my head—the one that beat down my self-esteem.

"Hey! You don't look so good today."

"You dummy, why would you do that?"

"You're not good enough."

That voice came back to me with a vengeance.

"I should be more than I am. I should have been a better father, a better husband, a better brother, a better friend."

The list was endless, and I had to sit on the bow as my mind unloaded its burden and my heart broke as I saw and understood my own mortality. The dam had broken, and I let the memories flood in. I didn't even try to hold in my emotion. Drop by drop the memories burned my eyes and flowed down my cheeks. They flooded from my breath and my poured from my sobs like a kick in the gut from a mule. My mistakes tore at my soul. I yearned for forgiveness from everyone, from anyone. I wanted someone to just say, "I love you. It's okay." A hug, a kiss, a touch. But none found me. My heart ached at the loss of time, friends, family and love. I felt terribly alone.

My tears landed on *Willow*, my quiet sobs resounded against her skin. The wind blew a quick gust, a kiss. I forced a smile and rested my forehead against her. I heard my keeper's strong voice, as He stood in this current of emotional pain. He did not shout over the noise of the memories or the voices, or the noise of the pain.

He merely whispered, "Forgive yourself."

I collapsed on *Willow's* deck, quietly in much emotional pain. She rocked ever so gently. And for the first time in my life, I forgave myself. I didn't look for excuses. I didn't look for reasons. I didn't look for answers. I just accepted me for who I am. I wasn't too young, or too dumb, or this or that. I only was. The abscess that was my past was lanced and the pressures of regret, loss and emptiness slowly drained away.

I rolled onto my back and looked up at the dark sky. I laughed and smiled and shook my head saying to myself, "53."

"It took you 53 years to learn this?"

"No. No, that's wrong. It took up until five minutes ago. What really matters is the last five minutes, not the 53 years before it."

It actually had only taken five minutes. Because, up to that point, I had never known that I *could* forgive myself, let alone how. Game changer. Life changer.

I lay there for a short while, wading through the memories, one leading to another. Some were good, others not so good, but they all pulled on my heart strings. I came away from the experience with a better understanding, a better meaning of me, my life and where I was.

I had planned on staying the night. I was not sure I could do it. Though dark at this day's end, the waterfront was brightly lit, and I decided I could go as far as the lights would allow. I started the motor with the pull cord, hauled in the anchor, turned on the navigation lights and headed back into the intracoastal. I hung a long sweep to port. The memories still fresh in my mind, faces attached to feeling, emotions left unchecked for decades.

I concentrated on the things around me. I forgave myself without judgement for not staying. At the same time, I promised that I would return in the near future to stay the night to truly come to terms with my past. I knew that I would. I was at peace.

About that time came a triple mast, wooden, Tall ship. She was stunning to watch as she glided through the water. Her colors flew atop the tall, wooden mast. I silently wished that they would unfurl the sails. That would have been a breathtaking sight.

I imagined myself its Captain.

"Aye! Hoist the sails mates! We're headed out for a long one. Best batten down the hatches and break out the good stock of rum. There she blows! Land Ho!"

Yeah, I always wanted to be a pirate, but a good one! I can dream.

Motoring along the intracoastal was like riding around in a car with the family looking at Christmas lights. These lights, nonstop on both sides, made for easy navigation (that is until the sky went dark directly in front of me.)

I couldn't understand why it had gone dark until I saw the light of the buoy next to me reflect off the black hull of a massive, fifty-eight story high, three hundred football fields, long-ass ship which had been pulling out in front of *Willow* for the prior ten minutes. And it was only about twenty yards away from me.

"Ho, ho, ho, no, no, no..."

I cranked hard on the vise grips to the starboard side, but
not sharply enough. I jumped back to the motor and turned it

as quickly and gently as possible. On a dime, she turned out of harm's way. For a moment, we motored quietly side by side. The giant ship's crew never knew we were there. I could have leaned out and touched it. I slowly motored *Willow* away from the massive vessel, and we motored alongside but at a safe distance. A tragedy avoided.

The large ship pulled away from me. I was at three quarters throttle. Fast enough for me. Soon, I was behind her. My heart pounds now, even as I write this months later.

When the ship had moved far enough away, I could see that she was a transcontinental cargo ship from China. I couldn't imagine how much her fuel bill is per day. Wow. Soon following behind her, I enjoyed the scenery.

More and more military ships with their American flags appeared. Brightly lit numbers marked each one. The last one was 75. Passing them created a chest-swelling, patriotic moment for me. I motored over and out of the way. It was the end of the line for the day. I had reached the Norfolk Tunnel, and beyond that would be the Chesapeake Bay.

I tossed the anchor, adorned the boom with the anchor light, and pulled up a bucket of salty water. I poured the cool, refreshing water over my head. I stripped down, washed my clothes, and washed myself.

Afterwards, I sat on the long bench sipping ice cold water and eating the last banana. Admiring America's might, remembering boot camp and mulling over the past made for an evening full of emotion. It the quiet night, I made my way into the bed and slept deeply.

Around 3 a.m. *Willow* rocked so violently from the port to starboard that it felt as my stomach was going to detach itself from my body. I had to spread my arms and legs out to keep from sliding back and forth. It went on for a good ten minutes and I could not move. *Willow* felt as though she was in the grasp of a giant's hands and it was shaking her to see what would fall out. When the rocking subsided, I slid down off the bed to make sure all things were still in place. I was shaken up a bit and I noticed the culprit fleeing the scene disguised as another massive tanker making its way north into the Chesapeake Bay.

***

DAY SIX

YOU'LL NEVER DO A WHOLE LOT,
UNLESS YOU'RE BRAVE ENOUGH TO TRY.
DOLLY PARTON

I woke while it was still dark out, jumped down from my bunk and made my way into the cockpit. Excited, I thought I could make it home to my parents' house by that night.

I got out the frying pan and fired up the propane stove. I also started the stovetop espresso maker and set about making eggs and cheese while I cut up and munched on the last slices of avocado. The five eggs finished cooking, I took the pan and coffee out to the cockpit and stood in my door eating out of the pan and sipping the rich coffee as I watched the glorious sunrise. Everything tasted better, smelled better and I breathed it all in deeply.

"This is it," I thought to myself, "this is the life."

Laughing aloud, I washed the utensils, tied the rope to the pan's handle and tossed it over the side. I removed my clothes from the line and dressed myself for the day. Shorts.

"That's it! What a way to live."

After cleaning up, I pull-started the motor. She started easily and as she warmed up, I pulled the anchor and scanned the horizon.

"Hmmm. Not much wind, but I see a storm out in the bay past the Norfolk Tunnel."

Excited, I wanted to catch the wind. I set a course for the Chesapeake Bay and the storm. While motoring along, I could see where the tunnel dove beneath the water. A simmering, vivid memory of me at the age of 19 bubbled to the surface—a picture of the tunnel entrance blocked by cars backed up in a standstill. At that time, I was the culprit. My old, blue ragtop Spitfire had died just as I had entered the tunnel at rush hour, making me and everyone behind me late for work.

Like my previous visits to Virginia Beach, I drove that car like an oversized go kart, zipping in and out of highway cones and fracturing speed limits. This day was no exception. I felt invigorated until the car sputtered and shook just as I began to enter the tunnel. I moved the stick shift into neutral and continued to coast towards the bottom. Try as I did, she wouldn't turn over. I tapped on the fuel gauge. The needle showed just under a quarter a tank. My heart sank as I coasted to the bottom and came to a slow stop.

Headlights flashed and horns honked behind me, people's shrill voices barely audible as I still tried to start the car, my face flush with embarrassment. In frustration, I grabbed the wheel and shook it, hoping that she would snap out of it.

"Come on baby, don't let me down."

She gave no response over the deafening noise inside the tunnel. I only noticed the tow truck when it was almost to me. The driver jumped out.

"Stay in the car," he shouted, "and put your car in neutral after I hook up to you."

I nodded. In minutes, I was being towed out of the tunnel. I noticed a black POW sticker on the back window and a sticker that said, "Vietnam Veteran."

He dropped me off in a small parking lot and unhooked my car. I asked what I owed him, gruffly.

"Nothing, it's my job."

I thanked him as I popped the hood, but she just wouldn't start. I tried everything I could. The tow truck driver had parked about five spaces away and watching me. He climbed out of his truck and walked over to me and offered me a gas can.

"Thank you, but it shows almost a quarter of a tank. It's never done this before," I said.

"The gauge could be broken," he said.

I nodded in agreement. Opening the gas cap made a hissing sound then stopped.

"Vapor lock," he said handing me the gas can.

"Here. Go ahead, take it just to make sure you get to where you are going. I've another can in the wrecker. No big deal." he added.

I poured the gas into the tank and reached for my wallet.

"Your money's no good to me. I bet she'll start right up," he said. I sat in the car and turned the key. Nothing. I looked at him and shrugged as I noticed the Navy Veteran cap he wore.

"Try again," he said.

"Need to get fuel to the carb."

With a second turn of the key she sprang to life. I jumped out of the car stretched out my hand and shook his.

"Thank you, thank you so much," I said.

He spat on the ground, turned his back to me and walked away. I had found it oddly strange that he could be so helpful yet so gruff at the same time. He may have seen his own mortality in me.

Later that day I was written up for dereliction of duty and disrespect of a non-commissioned officer for being late and I got busted down to an E2. My NCO said he didn't believe the excuse I had. After the Captain's Mast, I saw the NCO before I shipped to my next duty station and told him that my account of my delay had been the truth. He smiled, said, "I know," and turned and walked away. I later discovered that my punishment had been over a girl we both knew—the soon to-be mother of my children.

Returning from my daydream memory, we motored towards the storm through what appeared to be slightly rough waters. I set the autopilot and moved forward towards the mast to raise the mainsail.

"It doesn't look too bad," I thought.

But as I unhooked the halyard from its keep, the boat lurched causing me to grab the mast for support. In doing so, the halyard line became hung up on the side stay that sticks out from the mast some twenty feet above my head on the starboard side. I held onto the mast as I leaned out trying to whip the line free from the stay.

Willow entered the squall (that's what we call them.) The squall hit, and it hit hard. I almost slipped overboard as she plunged into a wave. Grabbing the mast, I wrapped both arms around it, clutched the loose halyard and looked forward as the wave washed over me, the deck and the cabin. I was grateful that the autopilot was doing its job. I didn't think I could make my way back to the safety of the cockpit as the squall reached its peak, plummeting rain and harsh wind with a harder burst. *Willow* dove deep into the waves head on, bucking wildly as my heart pounded and I gasped for air, screaming, "Wahoo!" or "Ohhh, shit!" over and over as she plowed into the waves.

"This is the absolute best rollercoaster ride of my life. I can see where Captain Dan was coming from," I thought.

I hung on elated, never once scared. I was in good hands (which both knew better than to let go.) My whole body took the impact of the water. I enjoyed it though it ripped my shorts down to my ankles.

I made a few attempts to pull them up, and I did manage to once, but gave up when the waves pulled them back down. Laughing, screaming, hollering, and buck naked, I held onto the mast in the middle of a squall never having felt so alive.
My body couldn't decide if it was cold or hot. Giving me a strange but enjoyable experience, the cold rain and wind made me shiver but the warm waves washed over me and warmed me again. Forty minutes passed before the squall had calmed enough for me to pull up my shorts. What a blast!

It took some effort, but I managed to untangle the mainsail line and clipped the halyard to the mainsail.

However, the top six feet of the mainsail were not connected to the mast. I studied it and tried to put the sail clips back into the rail on the mast.

"No can do," I realized.

I laid on the deck and finally figured it out. Pulling the small pin at the bottom of the mast rail, I pushed the entire sail down as I took all of the clips out of the rail. This was no easy feat as *Willow* continued to buck and dive. Luckily the wind had died down and the waves shrunk. I didn't mind the slacking rain. It felt refreshing.

Once I freed the sail and clips, I began with the top of the sail and the first clip, threading the clips one after the other until they were all in their proper place and sequence. Reinserting the small pin, I tightened up the main sail's line, moved to the cockpit and began to pull on the line to raise the mainsail. It suddenly stopped short. It would not raise anymore. I looked up expecting to see a fouled line or something. At first, I couldn't see anything wrong until I pulled on the line again.

With each tug, I could see the mainsail pulling the track from the mast about three quarters of the way up. About 8 feet of the sail track had all but fallen. The top half appeared secure, but the bottom half was off. I lowered the mainsail and secured it to the boom. Grateful for the motor, I returned to my spot in the cockpit.

I checked on the gas can and shook it.

"It's getting empty. She's at about a quarter of a tank. I'll give her a bit longer, then I'll switch tanks," I thought.

The round igloo cooler was empty, but I was not concerned about it at all. Yan had showed me the thirty gallons of potable water, so I put ice in my cup and went into the hot cabin. I set the cup down to go open up all three hatches to help ease the heat. Back at the sink, I pushed on the foot pump and took a big swig and immediately spit it into the sink.

It wasn't the taste that made me react that way. Something in the water slid over my tongue. I looked into the cup. Lying on the ice was a dark, greenish, worm-like creature.

"Oh, hell no! Yuck!"

I spat into the sink again. Since I couldn't rinse my mouth out, I grabbed my toothpaste and toothbrush. I went out into the cockpit to brush my teeth and gather my wits while I cursed and spit toothpaste over the side trying not to gag.
I considered the situation. No water for the rest of the day or the next.

"Fine. I can do that," I said to myself. Knowing full well I didn't want to.

I leaned over the side, rinsed my toothbrush in the salt water, and brushed my teeth again. Going back into the cabin I put up the toothbrush and grabbed my glasses to take a look at this worm or this thing (whatever it was.) It was about 5 inches long and not moving. The parts I had spat out were not moving either. Taking a closer look, I touched it and it kinda smeared. Not a worm at all. Algae.

"Okay, I feel better already," I murmured.

I pushed on the foot pump again and more algae came out. I wondered why it had not happened before. Then I realized that it probably had, but because it was dark when I washed the utensils...

"Crap!"

I went to the cockpit and pulled in the rope that was attached to the frying pan. To my relief it was clean, so I dried it and put it away. I stuck my head out to make sure our course was clear. Returning to the cabin I went to sort out the water situation. I was thirsty and didn't want to wait two days to quench it. I pulled a water tank. There were five of them, like the old, big gas cans but blue. I removed the cap and looked inside. Yup, inside on the bottom are blobs of algae.

"Cool."

I set the water can up on the step and poured myself a full cup, watching the whole time to make sure the algae stayed in the bottom. Taking a sip, I thought, "Yep, not bad," and just like that, the water crisis was over.

I looked at the map and judged that I could possibly make it to my parents' house that night. The long turn at the Virginia/Maryland border was only a few hours away. Once I made that turn, I'd be home free.

I shook the gas can. Time to switch tanks. I quickly unhooked the fuel line from one tank, connected it to the other and squeezed the bulb a few times. The motor never missed a beat.

The storm had broken, and it was turning out to be a scorcher. The wind against me, I couldn't even raise the jib. I could see quite a few sailboats in the distance leisurely sailing about though none strayed too far from the area. Motoring into the fray of sailboats, I had just passed a marker surrounded by large rocks in the middle of the sailing lane when *Willow* became silent. My heart sank. The motor died.

Embarrassing? A bit, but it happens right?

"Must have gotten some air in the line when I switched tanks. No big deal."

I judged that I had time to get the motor started before the wind pushed *Willow* into the rocks. I removed the motor cover, squeezed the bulb in the gas line a few times, wrapped the rope around the flywheel and pulled. Nothing. I wrapped the rope around the flywheel again and this time I pulled much harder, smashing my little finger and bending back the fingernail again in the process. (Yes, of course, the same little finger I'd hurt before.)

Clenching my fist to ease the pain, I wrapped the rope again using only my other hand. I saw a spot where the rope didn't quite fit under at the back of the flywheel, but I ignored it. My gut knew better. By then, the wind was pushing *Willow* towards the rocks. My smart hand hurt as my concern grew.

"I need this motor to start now!"

I leaned over and pulled hard on the starter rope with the other hand. It pulled for a moment then stopped as the remainder of the rope flew off, slapping me in the face and jarring my shoulder.

"That's why I don't let you do anything by yourself!"

With both hands in pain, I wrapped the rope around again and pulled. Nothing. Again, and again I tried, sweating profusely and red-faced, I could feel my heart beating in my ears.

The closer *Willow* drifted to the rocks, the faster I repeated the process. The third time, I hit the bulkhead with my hand again. It felt like I broke a finger. I threw the starter rope down and marched for the anchor locker on the bow. I retrieved the anchor, tossed it forward as best I could and tied it off.

Exhausted, I had no more strength. I grabbed the long cushions and laid on the upper deck under the boom in the scorching heat. The breeze made tolerable the little shade I had. Soon the heartbeat in my ears faded. I stopped sweating, fell asleep and did not move for about three hours.

When I woke up around six, I was grateful that the heat of the day had moved on. For the first time on this trip, I became concerned, afraid that something might be wrong with the motor that I couldn't fix. At this point, I couldn't sail and without use of the motor I would need to ask for help.

I climbed down from the deck and stowed the cushions away. Grabbing my cup, I poured a big cup of water (eyeballing the algae) and set about tinkering with the motor. I pulled the spark plugs and held onto it as I pulled the starter rope.

"Ouch! Dammit, yup," I said, shaking my hand.

"Still plenty of spark."

"Air? Why yes, there's plenty of air."

"Fuel. That had to be it."

I unscrewed the gas cap as it hissed while the can flexed into its original shape.

"Aha! Vapor lock!"

I screwed the cap back on, reinstalled the spark plugs, hooked up the spark plug wires, pumped the fuel bulb, wrapped the rope around the flywheel and pulled. Nothing. Nada.

Frustrated, I tried again and again. Like the dictionary definition of insanity, expecting different result each time, I tried again but my finger found the bulkhead and bent backwards. I threw the rope down as I grasped both hands together and jumped up and down, hollering with increasing anger, "Shit, shit, shit!"

I had forgotten that I was not completely alone and looked up as a beautiful sailboat cruised by not twenty yards away. I could see its occupants sipping red wine as they watched me. I saw their toast and read their lips:

"I'm so glad we're rich," they seemed to say.

"I'll bet you are," I thought to myself. "I'll bet you are."

I dug around and found the troubleshooting pages in the manual for the outboard motor. I read the first thing that I saw.

"If motor becomes submerged, do not attempt to start. Take it to the nearest Yamaha dealer for evaluation."

I really laughed at this.

"Sure thing, I'll get right on it."

I stepped my way through the entire troubleshooting list. If it's doing this, check that and so on. I even bypassed parts and fuses, trying each possible remedy it listed. She just would not start.

My feet were becoming oddly tender making it painful to walk, so much so that I threw the cushions from the bench seats onto the cockpit floor but that barely eased the pain. I continued to read more about maintenance and service on the motor and there, in a single sentence at the end, I found the problem: contaminated fuel. I shook my head.

"That couldn't be it. Could it?"

It made sense. I had spark, I had air, (I had removed the air filter just to be sure), and I had filled the gas tanks a few hours before. I disconnected the gas can, pulled it into the cockpit and set it on the bench seat. I removed the gas cap and peered inside. The gas didn't look bad and it smelled like gas. Then I saw water sloshing around the bottom.

"And where does the pickup tube sit? On the bottom." Feeling better, my frustration turned to hope. I checked the other gas tank and I couldn't see any water in it. I poured gas from another can into the tank, hooked it up and stowed the cans.

I unscrewed the brass screw on the motor carburetor, squeezed the fuel bulb and watched the water drain from the brass screw. When the white fuel turned to clear, I gave the bulb a few more squeezes just for good measure.

I pulled the choke, wrapped the rope around the flywheel and pulled. Nothing.

"But this had to be it."

Again, and again I tried. On the fourth go around she purred to life.

"Yes, yes, yes. Thank you, thank you!"

Almost jumping in the air with elation, I put the cover on the motor and let her warm up while I poured a bucket of salty water on my head to cool down. I looked around at all the sailboats, I'd say fifty at least. Many had sailed close by to take a peek, but none had asked or offered me help. If I had been sailing a forty foot, hundred thousand-dollar boat you betcha they would have stopped just to be polite.

My experience had taught me that people with money like doing business with people with money. I wouldn't have accepted any help anyway, but it would have been nice to have been asked.

My feet were hypersensitive, probably sunburned on the bottoms, so with the outboard running, I practically tiptoed to the bow and hoisted up the anchor. Gingerly, I made my way to the cockpit, put her in gear and motored away from the group of sailors.

I had lost about six hours all together but looking at the map I was still hopeful I could make home by night. I just needed to get around the big curve of the Virginia coastline. I figured around ten o'clock. It would get dark around nine so I could still make it (or so I thought.)

Around six, I set the autopilot and went forward to the wide bow with a bucket on a rope and the small brush. I gave the deck of her bow a bath. *Willow* had to be nice and clean to meet my family. Scrubbing the deck with one hand while keeping my feet in the shade and balancing painfully with my other hand was quite a challenge. After a few hours the sky became blackened dark. Grey clouds covered the moon.

I still had not reached the end of the big turn though I was dodging crab pots and pound nets, and really enjoying watching large ships way in the distance. The crab pots were becoming more and more difficult to spot.

"Just a bit further, "I thought.

I was looking at a large ship way out in front of *Willow* and it seemed odd. Something wasn't right. My eyes were focused not onto a faraway ship, but a pound net right in front of us. I panicked, turning the rudders hard left. I rushed to the motor, turned her too quickly and it stalled. I scrambled to the bow, pulled the anchor out and sprinted aft to toss the anchor back as far as I could.

It pulled hard, slowing *Willow* in the process. I knew if she hit the pound net it would be a huge mess, not to mention costly to repair of both the pound net and *Willow*. She slowed to a stop a mere few feet from the net. Pulling on the anchor, she swung around. I tied off the anchor and painfully made my way back to the cockpit. I stared at the pound net. It was at least a hundred-foot long with large posts driven into the bottom a little more than a foot apart. The poles, about six inches in diameter, stuck up above the water about eight feet. A stout set up, it probably wouldn't have given much if *Willow* had run into it. I could see the fishnet hanging from each pole, *Willow's* back a mere ten feet away.

I didn't care. I couldn't stand the thought of my sore feet making their way to the bow another time. I grabbed the anchor light, clipped it to the boom, grabbed a cup of water and went to bed.

***

DAY SEVEN

THE TWO MOST IMPORTANT DAYS OF YOUR LIFE ARE
THE DAY THAT YOU'RE BORN AND
THE DAY YOU FIND OUT WHY.
MARK TWAIN

Through an uncomfortable, painful night my feet throbbed, my shoulder and arm ached, and God helped me through the pain every time the sheet laid on my hand. (You remember, the hand that I had tenderized on the bulkhead.) Rolling over and repositioning myself to get comfortable was totally out of the question. I didn't get any sleep. I just dozed between the pain and the cramps. When morning broke, I slowly made my way out of the bed. I knew I was in trouble when my feet touched the floor.

I couldn't put any weight on them because I had burned the bottoms and they blistered. I swung myself from the bed over to the toilet to sit, and that took most of the weight off of them. I wanted to crawl back into bed, but I knew I would still have to suffer the same fate later anyway. So, there I sat, like a man without a country, on his throne in his home in the middle of nowhere. I pushed down with my feet and then let them up, working them to try to release the fluid.

I thought about the fishermen who worked the pound net just aft of *Willow*. I had done no damage at all, but I didn't want to be there when they came back to work. After about fifteen minutes, I gently stood up. Both feet hurt like hell, barely tolerable. I needed to get underway. I slapped open the saloon doors, slid the hatch back and carefully stepped out into the cockpit.

I removed the anchor light and placed it next to the rum. The cushions I had scattered on the cockpit floor the day before helped to lessen the pain to just under tolerable. I removed the cover from the motor and in two pulls, she was up and running. I waddled my way to pull the anchor, left it on the deck and waddled my ass back like a three hundred-pound goose to stand on the cushions.

I put the motor in gear, made a long passing sweep around the big pound net, and set a course for Saint George's Island. I still had to complete the big turn for what I figured would be a few hours of dodging crab pots and pound nets before I reached the Maryland state line.

Once I hit the state line, I thought that I was coming out of the big turn, but a few hours later, I still hadn't rounded it, imagining the land had probably been incorrectly sized on the map. Finally, yet a few more hours later, I was ready to cut across and make a beeline towards home.

Excitedly I set about cleaning *Willow*. I went through the cooler and put everything I had not eaten into a trash bag. I went into the cabin and packed my suitcase. All of my clothes were soaked from a leak in the cabin hatch, so I put my dirty clothes, sheets, blankets and pillows cases into another trash bag.

Completely beside myself with anticipation I thought, "A shower. Yes, I want a nice hot shower! And to see my mom, dad and brother and to be able to hug them."

Motoring east of St. George's Island, I decided to return home in style to the degree that I could. Another squall had been chasing *Willow* and I could feel the wind pick up. Moving carefully up to the bow I grabbed the jib pole and unfurled the jib. She blossomed as the wind filled the sail.

I stood back behind my vise grip steering wheel, dodging crab pots with ease. When I saw where the old Lumpkin's Seafood House used to be and the small bridge that connected it to Piney Point, I knew I was close. It felt like home. I saw the Harry Lundeberg School of Seamanship and tears filled my eyes, my heart full of so many good memories.

I spied the flash of familiar headlights in the park just before the bridge.

"Mom! Dad! Jonathan!"

My parents and my brother were all there waving. Still some distance away, I grabbed a shirt and waved it frantically above my head while shouting to the top of my lungs,

"I MADE IT, I MADE IT!"

Hollering, waving all the way past them, my tears flowed. My heart hurt. I had not realized how much I missed them. I had only been at sea for seven days, but you would have thought I had been lost, missing for years. I wished that my sister, my kids, everyone—I wished everyone could have been there. I missed them all terribly.

I passed the school and I let out the jib so it would wind back up, moving forward to give it a little help. When putting up the pole, I tripped and almost hit the water. Instead, I hit the deck hard. I looked back, hoping that no one had seen me. Fortunately, they had already left to meet me at the house.

Shaking it off, I took *Willow* on a long sweep starboard and motored into the cove of Andover Estates, the home of my childhood. I smiled through my streaming tears. In the distance I saw my brother walk to the end of the dock. He's taller than me and lean. I'd missed him too. He was my unknowing savior out on the boat.

The squall had reached *Willow*, but without much wind as the cove was good protection. But the rain drummed down. I had just passed the neighbors pier when I went to the motor to slow it down. I eased up on the throttle and she died like the perfect end to a tragedy.

"Oh, my God! Really? Hell no! This ain't happening! Not here, not now!"

But it did.

The wind, finding its way to *Willow*, began to push her back the way we had come. I made my way to the bow.

"Are you ok?" my brother Jonathan called.

"Yeah, the motor died. Give me a minute. I'm sorry. Y'all go on inside, I'll be there shortly," I hollered.

Mom called back, "We're okay. We're going to wait for you."

"God, I love that woman," I thought aloud.

I made my way back to the motor, removed the cover, pumped the fuel bulb, wrapped the rope around the flywheel and pulled. She fired up and died as soon as I put it in gear. This happened a few times. Frustrated, I jammed it in gear and gave it gas at the same time.

I never expected the motor's reaction. That little motor goosed so hard that it not only twisted the metal bracket, but it also bent it until it collapsed! This allowed the propeller to spin as it pointed straight up at the boat. The motor fully prone, looked like it was tanning on a beach while the back of the motor barely touched the water. I pulled the emergency stop cord and stared at the engine. It looked and felt like it mocked me:

"How'd you like that?"

"Whatcha gonna do now?"

"How 'bout that, huh?"

"How 'bout this?" (I imagined reaching my foot over and stomping on the outboard motor again and again until the little monster let go of my girl *Willow* and sank to the bottom.)

"How you like that, huh?" I'd say.

(I didn't actually do it. My feet were hurting too much, but I sure thought about it…)

Instead, I turned and went forward to the anchor and gave it a toss. I hollered to Mom and Dad that it might be a while and instructed them to get out of the rain.

"Okay, see you soon," they called as they both went inside as the rain started coming down.

I watched them go, leaning on each other all the way up and inside. I knew it had to be painful for my dad to walk down to the pier. Jonathan was already heading my way in the canoe.

Once he got close enough, he jumped out of the canoe and into the cockpit.

"Nice!" he said.

"Yes, she is. She's just trying to test me, wanting to make sure I truly want her," I replied.

In typical form he retorted, "Like a woman? How'd that work for you last time?"

"Yeah. Good point."

We both laughed.

"Alright, how…Holy crap! How'd that happen?" he asked, looking at the motor on its back.

"It's a long story. I need to pull the motor up with the pulley on the boom, unhook the bracket from both the motor and transom and then remount the motor back into its original position."

Jonathan and I worked easily together, talking and laughing. I reminisced of years back when he had come to work with me, to help me with one of my first companies; truly one of the best times of my life. I missed it and I had missed him. We let life get in the way and we each took separate paths.

After about an hour working to reset the motor, along with another hour of laughing at old memories, I tried again, but she just wouldn't start. Jonathan stood on the bow waiting to pull up the anchor whenever the motor finally decided to start.

The motor would not start that day. He finally decided to play "Anchor Toss", pulling *Willow* the last thirty yards home. When we were close enough, Jonathan jumped onto the dock and tied off *Willow*. I began unpacking, setting the trash, clothes and food on the dock, along with the bottle of wine and my brother helped me carry it all up to the house.

I had hoped to make a grand entrance, as if I knew what I was doing, like I was a sailor. I wanted to be *that* guy. To me I had failed miserably. To my family I was *that* guy, and that's all that mattered.

As soon as I finally crossed home's threshold, a cascade of tears flowed as I hugged them all. It was an amazing moment. The hugs, the tears, the laughter. Words from them all.

"You did it!" they said.

"I can't believe you made it! That's amazing, especially considering you've never sailed before!"

"You are definitely the Viking in the family."

"Whoop Whoo! So glad you're home!"

Opening the bottle of wine, I poured each one a glass.

"A toast!

"To our Viking!"

And that was before I told them this story.

***

Enjoy your life. There will be some risks. Enjoy those too! ~ Jason Boyd

AFTERWORD

The day after I had the migraine, I decided not to take my medication. Shortly after I had arrived home, I went to the bedroom and weighed myself. I had lost fifteen pounds! I retrieved my kit and checked my blood sugar; 127. This was huge! Normally, my blood sugar runs around 450-500 without medication. *Willow* was literally going to save my life.

After the initial excitement of coming home and regaling my family with the mishaps of my adventure, I rang Yan to let him know I had made it safely home and to share the story with him.

During that touching conversation, I laughed a lot. Yan...not so much. He kept saying how terrible he felt about the troubles I had encountered, and I could feel his angst through the phone. I told him I'd just lived one of the greatest adventures of my life, that I would not change the experience one bit. More important than the wild events of each day had been the effect the trip had on my soul, for which I remain grateful. We said our goodbyes promising to keep in touch.

Yan called me a few hours later and offered to send me a substantial amount of money for my troubles. He asked that I send an email to his wife with my info and I said I would. We said goodbyes once again and hung up.

I went back to the bedroom and flopped down, ready to send him my particulars. I couldn't do it. The money was of no consequence. The adventure, Yan, *Willow,* and I were more valuable than money. I would not cheapen our worth or damage our connection. I wanted to strengthen it the only way I knew how; by being honest. So, I wrote a letter and sent it to Yan's wife.

Hello,

It was a pleasure meeting you last week during the purchase of *Willow*. I don't know if Yan has shared my adventure with her, but knowing him, I'm sure he has. I know you have a lot on your plate and I'm sure I'm not going to tell you anything you don't already know so let me get down to the brass.

Like I told Yan, I knew that I was going to buy the sailboat before I even got off the plane. When he took me to meet *Willow*, I was more interested in learning more about Yan and his experience than in the purchase of *Willow*. To me, it was a done deal. I am rich by no means, nor even that well off. I've saved for years to have the money available to make such a large purchase. It was huge and scary, I'll have to admit.

What I'm getting at, I felt Yan was a good man, honest with his words and his sincerity. I could feel it. At the bank, I watched you two very closely. And it solidified my assumptions to truth. The small gestures and the looks between y'all, showed me a great love the two of you share. I knew I had bought the right sailboat from the right man.

In spite of all the mishaps, pain, LOL, and suffering, I appreciate his offer to return some of the purchase price back to me. During our conversation I knew he was going to do that. Because, he is THAT man, that guy, that hero. That, I feel we all strive to be. And at the same time, I knew that I could not accept such a gift. Like I explained to him, there was never ever any doubt in my mind that he was honest with me in every way. He was true to his word to the fullest extent of his knowledge of the condition of *Willow*. And, as you already know, he's truly one of a kind.

So, I respectfully, and admirably, decline the refund of monies. Just the thought was gift enough. I truly appreciate the gesture. I know this probably will hurt his feelings a bit, and I do get it. But it is not a rejection of his offer, I've come to realize a better compromise, if he will accept. It's something that I hope will help us both. Even if he declines my counter offer, I do not wish any money having to do with *Willow*.

I know he explained to me that he feels somewhat useless because of his blindness. I believe that he can help me, and in doing so, will also help himself. I am going to write about the adventure on *Willow* and record it so he can listen to it in hopes that he will be compelled to share his own adventures with the world. Nobody knows how far their bloodline will go. But someone down the line will wonder, what were my great Grandpa and Grandma like?

Answer the question for generations with your own words. I can't imagine the stories he's acquired over the years. It's about sharing stories, making people dream, lifting their imagination. There are too many stories left untold, due to being placed in the ground. There is always a way if you want to do something. And, upfront and foremost he is worthy, as are the stories.

It is such a pleasure to have met such an original individual. I know it was a bit longer than even I anticipated, sorry about that. Thank you for your time!

Truly,

Jason

Later that evening, just before bed, I sat on the couch in front of the picture window looking out into the backyard and the cove. There was my girl *Willow*, moored to the end of the pier waiting, ready to go again. At the approach to the dock stood the young willow tree, my writing bench tucked under her arms facing the water. Off to the left, like an unmarked grave, an empty space of grass held the place where the elder willow once stood which provides an explanation as to why I had to buy her.

These three willows each hold their own stories and adventures. Is there another *Willow* somewhere? Only time will tell.

I smiled and shook my head as I stared out at *Willow*. It felt like everything had been a dream. Was it real? My hand, my shoulder and my feet reminded me that yes, it was all too real. I hobbled off to bed and soon I slept hard, with barely a toss or turn. Home, the place where I'd always gotten the best sleep. Given my adventure it came as no surprise that I woke with the sun.

Normally, it was unusual for me to be the first one out of bed. My mom is usually up before me and the smell of coffee and cooking breakfast fill the house. But on this morning, I made the coffee. After fixing my cup, I sat on the overstuffed couch facing the picture window. I took a sip and looked out. My heart leapt into my throat. I dropped the coffee and rushed to the window. Pushing my face against it, I looked to the left and right.

"This can't be."

Bolting from the window, I ran outside and onto the deck to look again at the empty pier.

Willow was gone!

I ran down to the pier in pain and a panic unable to comprehend the hows and whys. I reached the end of the pier. Nothing but open water to the right. I just couldn't wrap my head around it. Then I turned and looked left.

There she hid in the only corner of the cove that I couldn't see from the vantage point of the couch. Like a small child wanting to play hide and seek, *Willow* had gathered her new friends (the canoe and my brother's catamaran) and hid in the corner. I was so focused on *Willow*, I hadn't noticed them missing too. A sigh of relief escaped me followed by laughter.

"Yes, you got me," I said loud enough for her to hear.

It felt as though the three were giggling at me. I smiled and shook my head.

"She's already a bad influence with the other boats. My kinda girl," I thought.

I left her to spend time with her new friends as I headed to the house to clean up my mess and get another cup of coffee. It was going to be one of those days.

I enjoyed breakfast and coffee with my mom and dad, answering their questions about the adventure and recalling details that I had overlooked earlier. Added to the story was the morning's moments of panic I'd had during *Willow's* hide and seek. We all had a good laugh. I'm still baffled how she was able to get them all untied and grouped together.

After breakfast, Dad and I headed to the local Dysons hardware store for aluminum rivets to repair the top sail track on the mast. Once home, I put on my shorts and water shoes and headed out the door to retrieve *Willow* and friends. With fear written on her face, my mom stopped me to ask if there was any other way to gather the boats.

Mom had good reason to worry. When my dad had gotten a scratch on his leg while in the water working on the pier, a bacterial infection set in his leg which caused him months in the intensive care unit. It had nearly cost him his life.

"There is no other way," I explained.

I promised her I would shower and use bleach to kill off any of the bacteria as soon as I was done. This seemed to ease her fear but did little to assuage my own. I never let on how truly scared I felt about going into the bacteria-infested water. If I got an infection, the diabetes would make battling it difficult.

Reaching the end of the pier, I sat on the edge feet first and slid slowly into the water. My feet touched the bottom. As I stood up, they sunk a good foot further into the muck where many a sneaker had been lost back in the day. I could feel gross, small things in the muck scraping against my legs. Like hungry little teeth, it reminded me of scraping the bottom of the boat and feeling of the worms. The thought still fresh in my mind, I shivered.

Becoming a little concerned, I half dog-paddled using my hands on the bottom as my feet floated behind me. I pulled the snickering canoe and my brother's giggling catamaran back to the pier and tied them off. When I returned to retrieve *Willow,* she wouldn't budge. I walked around to her rudders and pulled them up as high as I could tying them off hoping that was the cause.

"Nope, she's stuck fast."

I looked at the water lines along the shore and I was relieved to see the indications that low tide was upon us. I painfully climbed aboard and pulled out the anchor and all of its line. I tied off the end of the anchor line and got back in the water. Reaching up to grab the anchor, I carried it at an outward angle away from the boat as far as the anchor line would allow. Pulling it tight I shoved the anchor in the muck and stomped on it with all my weight sinking it so deep I could only feel the chain. Making my way back onto *Willow*, I tightened the anchor line with the mast winch so tight I could have walked it like a tightrope. I figured that as the tide came in, it would pull *Willow* free.

Then, I had nothing to do but take a bleach shower and wait. It was not pleasant. My legs stung from the many scratches, and if that wasn't unpleasant enough, scrubbing my body with a bleach-soaked, green scrubby that should be used on pots and pans made it terribly painful. But my fear of the bacteria outweighed the pain. So, I scrubbed.

At the end of the shower while drying off, I noticed the many tiny blood marks on the towel and threw it into the washer. I was not looking forward to getting back in the water or the shower later on.

While waiting on the tide I ordered a new starter spark plugs, an impeller and fuel filter for *Willow's* outboard motor online which would arrive two days later. I saw so many things for *Willow*, but I refrained from buying more and got off the computer. First things first.

When the high tide came, I made the trek to *Willow*. She seemed lonely, as if she longed to be near her newly found friends—so much in fact she easily became unstuck, as if it wasn't as much fun for her to taunt me as it had been in the beginning. The biggest problem was pulling the anchor out of the muck which I had to dig out with my hands. After about thirty minutes, the thick bottom released its mucky grip on the anchor. She made her way effortlessly back to the pier.

After tying off *Willow* I immediately took another painful shower. Afterwards I found myself staring out the big picture window, amazed that I survived the whole ordeal. I shook my head and snickered.

I did survive and I had never felt so alive, so thrilled, so fearful, and desperate at the same time. It was wonderful that I had found something in myself that I did not know I lost. To put it into words does not do the feeling justice, because it requires more than a simple explanation.

I will share with you, as best as I can, the feeling. Dare I say that I am more than I am? I feel that each of us are, that my (or our) full potential as human beings may never be realized unless we push the envelope. But in order to push the envelope, we must allow ourselves to feel.

Emotions are the truer things. The purest of life. I'm not talking of the money or success that society dictates. I'm talking of emotional success and the inner richness that we deny ourselves as we fear change that may carry with it pain. I implore you not to waste time. We all have so little. Time and love are of the utmost value.

As my tale nears its end, I feel compelled to share with you the hopeful future of *Willow* and me. To prepare, I replaced the starter, repaired the mainsail track, and completed all of the repairs myself. *Willow* should be ready to sail when I return to Maryland next year.

Today, I'm heading back home about an hour and a half drive south of Houston to Sargent, Texas, to shut down my businesses and remodel the house to be ready to rent.

Meanwhile in Sargent on most Fridays I'll walk out on Little Stubby, our shortest pier where we educate each other on the particulars of drinking beer and fishing while we take beautiful pictures of sunrises and sunsets. We are that drinking town with a fishing problem. And it shows, and I love it.

From Little Stubby, I do live updates for the members of Saving Sargent. I tell them how the weather and beach is looking, and how our new bridge is coming along (our swing bridge is being replaced with one of the ugliest bridges I've ever seen which I, along with a handful of locals, hate). I remind everyone about any upcoming events, and I give a shout out to people who have helped others. It's live so I do screw things up and embarrass myself a bit from time to time which makes it fun while keeping it real, almost like a live newspaper. Afterwards I get geared up for Friday night.

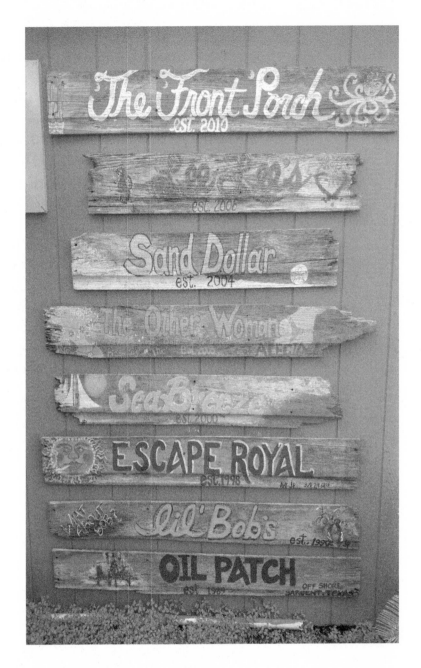

Until I leave, I plan to be playing and singing karaoke at the The Front Porch on Fridays and Saturdays with Donna and Craig, Gary, Jana, Henry, Paul, Heather R, Heather M, Brad, Marvin, Miranda, Anissa, Double D, Lorraine, Mark,

John and playing "Guess This Song" with Big D. I believe The Front Porch is the oldest bar in Sargent. It's probably the shortest in Texas. I have to duck a lot for its low ceilings and doorways but the owner Aleshia along with her crew Debbie C, Debbie A, Christy, Joey, Shannon and the people there like Susan, Peg, Mel, (yes! the On The Corner Girls!), Ralph, Vern, Rayanna, Sherry, Wild Bill, Jerry, Gina, Kenny, John, Shelly, Robert, Shelia, Don(Pappy), Roger, Kandas, Jessica, Lara, Winnie, Joey and Frank along with the many others that make it feel like home.

I always try to make it to breakfast at On the Corner (the oldest restaurant in Sargent) where the owner Jane, her daughter Susan along with Peggy, Mel and Soni (Slugger) are like family to me. Together they can change the disposition of even the grumpiest customer with their smiles, quick wit and just plain good, down-home cooking. Sunday breakfast buffet is my favorite. I truly enjoy visiting with the crew and George. Together, we have the most comical mornings.

George arrives like clockwork every morning at nine thirty. Me? Closer to ten just so I can visit more when fewer people are around because our conversations tend to get a little loud due to the joking around and laughter. I hardly watch TV. This pastime is more entertaining and uplifting. If you ever get by this sleepy coastal town be sure to stop by and say "hi" for me. You won't be disappointed. There are other newer restaurants and bars, but these are my favorite because they hold the best people, my favorite people.

I have fifteen years vested in this little coastal town, the longest I've lived anywhere. It's not perfect, but the people make it perfect enough for me, and I truly believe that I could never find another life like the one I have lived in Sargent. I have been truly blessed.

The town with its full timers, its weekenders, and its visitors come together when one of their own falls down and out. In saying that, Phil and Chelly Hardin, you both are still in my prayers.

I plan to leave Sargent in May 2019 to head home once again to Maryland, make a few modifications to *Willow* and sail her back to Texas. Stopping by New Bern to visit Yan. He has mentioned that he may want me to assist him in writing about his adventures which would be both a blessing and an honor. Yan is legend, I assure you.

Even though Yan is mostly blind, perhaps we will sail to the Bahamas together and create a new adventure. Maybe we will band together, keep a journal of our travels, and call it "Sailing Blind."

I will miss my life in Sargent, By Gawd, Texas. I do plan to return on *Willow*, I just don't know when it will be.

Love to all.

J

***

Special Thanks to the Following Facebook Groups. If this is your dream, you need to check out these guys! There are many more, but this is my top ten in no particular order. Interesting to watch videos and be able to ask questions. Thank you all for your help along this journey!

Prout Catamaran Owners
Champagne Boating on a Beer Budget
Sailboat Swap Shop
Liveaboard Sailboat
Living On The Hook
Sailors Helping Sailors
Wooden Boat Forum
Cruising and Living Aboard
Sailor Park Trash
Tiny Liveaboards (less than 33ft)

ABOUT THE AUTHOR

WHILE JASON BOYD AND HIS FAMILY CALL VALLEY LEE, MARYLAND HOME, HE HAS CLAIMED SARGENT, TEXAS AS HIS HOME FOR THE LAST FIFTEEN YEARS.

JASON ENJOYS SINGING AT SARGENT'S FRONT PORCH BAR, MAKING PEOPLE LAUGH AND LENDING AN EAR, SHOULDER, OR A HAND TO THOSE IN NEED, QUIETLY COUNSELING THOSE TRYING TO MAKE A BETTER LIFE. JASON STARTED WRITING AT THE AGE OF 12 AND IS CURRENTLY WORKING ON HIS NEXT PUBLICATION.

IN 2018, HE WAS AWARDED "MAN OF THE YEAR" FOR HIS ORGANIZATION OF THE FACEBOOK GROUP "SAVING SARGENT" WHICH PROVIDED HELP FOR MANY PEOPLE DURING HURRICANE HARVEY. THE GROUP CONTINUES TO HELP THOSE IN NEED.

Made in the USA
Coppell, TX
23 March 2022

75422604R00090